Moments with Joey

Jason Zimmerman

For the teachers who put up with me as a child, and to all of the Joeys that make this world a much more interesting place.

SCENES

	Introduction	7
	Prologue	10
1	Joey Dosen't Like Kittys	17
2	Profanity	20
3	Super Atomic Wedgies	23
4	Eye Doctors and Tooth Fairies	26
5	Vocabulary	28
6	Tracking Hilarity	30
7	Daylight Saving	36
8	Hot, Hotter, Hottest	39
9	Dreams and Nightmares	42
10	Resting Rooms	45
11	Can I?	46
12	Deep Thoughts	49
13	Annoying and Distracting	52
14	Life and Milk Cartons	55
15	The Wasp	58
16	The Dime	61
17	Entertainment Starved	64
18	Genes and Brains	67
19	The Pet	70

20	Inappropriateness	74
21	Music	77
22	Hard Work and Good Smells	80
23	Dream and Nightmares 2	82
24	Popularity	85
24	Unicorn Lockdown	88
25	Hotness	91
26	Camping Trips	94
27	Too Many Jokers, Not Enough Aces	97
28	Transformations	98
29	License to Drive	100
30	Geysers and Boysers	102
31	Belly Dancers and Roller Derbies	105
32	The New Student	112
33	Literature Responses	115
34	Unspoken Thoughts	118
35	Wasp Paste, Awesome Juice, and Hot Dogs	121
36	Competitions	124
37	Defense Mechanisms	127
38	Locked Rooms	130
39	The Greatest Gift	133
40	The Gift	136
41	The Tongue Dilemma	140

42	Just Checking	146
43	Mistaken Identities	148
44	Favorites	153
45	Brains	156
46	The Assignment	159
47	The Tooth	163
48	Pea Shooters	168
49	Problems	171
50	The Confession	174
51	Punishments	178
52	The Cellphone	181
53	Real Men	185
54	Diminishing Return	188

	Additional Quotes	191
	Afterword	196
	About the Author	197

INTRODUCTION

What a journey it has been to bring this collection to your hands.

Back in the summer of 2012 Jason took on a project to pull together his favorite Joey moments and adding new ones to publish as his first book. He spent the summer vacation quietly editing, emailing colleagues and friends for advice, put out requests for fun quotes, and asked a small group of people to edit what would finally become Moments With Joey.

Then the worst happened. Very few people were even aware of Jason's struggles with severe depression, and none of us were prepared for the depths that darkness would take. Jason lost his fight against depression and took his own life just weeks before he had planned to release this book.

I can hear you now, *Geez Shawna*, you sigh. *What a bummer of an opening act while ushering us to our front row seats.*

Yes, I can see how you feel there. The truth isn't always a bright or pretty thing, and, in all honesty, this isn't something I think I can sugarcoat or gloss over. Jason often felt unworthy of the praise that was given to him, and like he was an imposter posing as someone better than he actually was. Those of us who knew him were able to see just how good of a man he was, as he had a way of just lifting up a person's spirit with a smile, a joke, or a heartfelt offer of help.

As I have been putting the final touches on this manuscript I have, more than once, smiled at the first quote Jason chose to use for his book. I decided to keep it as is, but I think I may have to clarify my thinking a bit. You see, as dark as Jason's death was for those of us left behind, it opened us all to the fact that anyone can struggle with depression, thoughts of worthlessness, or be touched by the horror of a life ended far too young.

Darkness touched us all, and while I still miss my brother with every passing day, something else happened. I noticed I was not taking things for granted. I stopped worrying so much about my own little troubles. I started being much more grateful for the people around me and, rather than offering a token "how are you doing?" when talking with someone, I started listening completely and found myself being all the more sincere with my thoughts, words and deeds.

It may not sound like much, but I guess it comes down to trying to live a little more deliberately, rather than just idly watching time drift by.

I remember one of the last few conversations I had with Jason where he talked about having thought he had seen his last sunset and how he was now appreciating each new one he witnessed. As a result I now savor each sunrise and sunset, as they are each as varied and unique as we all are with one another.

This book is the start to a promise I made to have Moments With Joey published one day. That promise has expanded to see some of Jason's other works published as well, starting with My Brother Ryan, coming out next year. Jason always wanted to be a published author, and I think that excitement would still hold true for him in spirit as it did when he lived and breathed in body.

For those who likewise live with depression or thoughts of self-harm, please seek help. Do not be like my dear brother, who feared what others might think of him if they found out he was considering therapy or, heaven forbid, put on medication. There is no shame in asking for help, and it is never your fault that you have a medical condition requiring treatment, for this truly is a medical condition and cannot be merely wished away or ignored. In that vein I will be the first to stand up and admit that Yes, I too suffer from depression, and have tried suicide in the past. I sought help, and there is a light at the end of the tunnel. I am on medication, and probably will be for the rest of my life, but that life is certainly much easier and my melancholy swings far lighter for having faced my health issues head on.

The National Suicide Prevention Hotline is available 24 hours a day and can be reached toll free at **1-800-273-8255**. The call is anonymous and has no cost. You can also chat online and find helpful information at https://suicidepreventionlifeline.org

I hope that if presented with a new sunset, the chance to make a friend, or to deepen the bonds of a relationship you already cherish, that you hold on just that much more tightly and drink life in as deeply as you can. Dive in with your whole heart and stop holding back from pursuing your dreams. Life's situations may change, but you do not have to let those changes define who you are, your worth or your place in this wonderful world.

Shawna Zimmerman Gregg
November 2018

"Sometimes we are thrown a curve ball. We expect one thing out of life, and it gives us something completely different. Something better. Something we didn't expect, but we later find ourselves grateful for when we finally catch hold of it."

— Jason Zimmerman

PROLOGUE

I'm going start off by sharing a little secret with you, something I usually don't share with others. However, since we're going to be friends, I'm going to let you in on this little-known fact about me:

I hate it when I'm given a new book to read.

Okay, maybe *hate* is much too powerful of a word to use. Maybe what I mean is that starting a new book usually tends to make me feel... uncomfortable. I start reading the first page or two and I find myself completely lost. Who are these people? What in the world is going on? And most importantly, why should I even care? This feeling usually persists through the first ten to fifteen minutes, but occasionally can last longer. In these cases, I'll usually only persist for a few more minutes before unceremoniously stuffing the book back on the shelf and looking for something a little more familiar and comfortable to read.

Now, by admitting this, I hope I didn't put you under the impression that this little trait makes me someone who doesn't enjoy new experiences (or who is incurious), as nothing could be further from the truth! It's just that newness can be difficult at the very outset, and it's something that takes a little bit of getting used to.

Now, if you have ever felt this same way about the reading experience, this chapter should come as a form of comfort. This is the place where I'm going to clue you in, give you a little background, and set your worries at ease. By the time we've finished, I hope you'll feel like we're the best of friends (or at least more than complete strangers, as most of us are at the present moment).

It was Glenda, the good witch in the film The Wizard of Oz, who once so eloquently said, *"It's always best to start at the beginning..."* And like Dorothy, getting enough information to properly set out on her journey down the yellow brick road, this is the place where you'll better come to know who I am and just what this book is about. So, click your heels together three times and we'll be on our way!

I started off as a child.

That's not so surprising is it? Most of us start that way. While we may not remember all the experiences of yesteryear that helped to shape us into the individuals we are today, those experiences still happened. These things have become an innate part of us all. They are the things that have defined us.

Because of my own personal life definitions, I feel it necessary to tell you that I spent a vast majority of my childhood—and growing up—in a place called Summit Valley, Washington. It's one of those places that you've probably never heard of, but its name suggests what it might look like: large valley regions buried deep in the mountains of the Inland Northwest, where pine and aspen trees cover the steep slopes, overgrown with knotty clusters of Oregon grapes and wild roses. On a sweltering summer's day, you could smell the pitch from the pines permeating the air for miles around.

My family and I moved to Summit Valley when I was about six years old, and this was my first experience at attending a school that was a bit different than most conventional schools of the day. You see, because of the remoteness of the valley, the nearest town with a school was a half hour's drive away; therefore, the community had built a two-room schoolhouse in the heart of the valley, back before the turn of the twentieth century.

Alright, I feel it necessary that I stop your imagination right now; already I can see images of Laura Ingalls Wilder forming in your mind's eye. No, it wasn't at all like that. Sure, the schoolhouse had been built back in the late 1800s, but nobody rode to school in horse-drawn buggies, we didn't wear knickers, and we didn't write on slates with chalk.

The thing that most predominately set this school apart from many others of the day was the fact that it had only two classrooms, where students in first through sixth grades would attend. Because the community had such a sparse population, the number of school-aged children in the area was small as well. The first through third grades were housed in one classroom, while fourth through sixth grades were accommodated in the other. We had one teacher and an aide in each of these combined-aged classrooms.

Being raised in a rural farming community was something I soon became accustomed to while growing up. Getting up in the morning long before the light of day to milk seven goats before school was commonplace, and walking a half mile to catch the bus with my older sister was something I was used to. This understanding will help to illustrate why I had so few teachers during my elementary years.

While I loved and respected many of these teachers, a few of them just didn't quite understand the type of kid I was. I was recently digging through a box of memorabilia my mom had stored away over the years, and I stumbled across my old report cards. As I rifled through them and read over the anecdotal notes, I noticed a general trend: while I did satisfactorily with things such as being respectful and varied areas of mathematics, I struggled with reading, writing, focusing on the task currently at hand, and I had a general inability to follow through with instructions. In remembering back on some of my experiences of childhood, I realize that in today's world I would probably have been diagnosed as having ADD, ADHD, WXYZ, or any number of the other disorders. Back then, I was simply labeled as 'off task and talkative.'

One thing that my report cards never talked about was the other side of that 'off-taskness'. I—like many boys my age—was adventurous, imaginative, and maybe even just a little bit precocious. I had an imagination that just wouldn't quit, and I had a mind that was always working.

I was the kid you heard stories about. I was the boy who tied a blanket around his neck as a cape and leapt from the barn window in an attempt to fly. I was the kid who imagined the entire room tilting forward so the front wall was now the floor, and then played a movie through my head about what I would climb in order to reach the door—now at the top of the room. I was the kid who downed nearly an entire bottle of multivitamins in order to 'be strong' just as my mom told me I would be if I took them every day; I was also, consequently, the boy who then had to be driven to the hospital to get his stomach pumped. In other words, I was the kid with far too much imagination to be constrained by the space of that tiny little desk in a corner of the classroom. I was a kid with ideas that couldn't be held inside by sitting for far too long.

You know what the really funny thing is? You already know me. You see, I'm that kid you remember from back when you were in elementary school. I'm the kid who made you laugh during class, who talked when he wasn't supposed to, and—not trying to be a troublemaker—just had a little bit too much imagination for his own good. Like I said before, in today's society, I would simply have been labeled with a diagnosis and then (probably) medicated.

I can remember back to my sixth grade year in Otamay Hushing's classroom; one day she asked us all what we wanted to do with our lives. As my classmates and I pondered over this question, with thoughts that this was something-so-far-away-in-the-distant-future-that-it'll-probably-never-happen-to-us, two possibilities sprung to mind. In fact, I decided then and there what I was going to do with my life: I was either going to be a world-famous director/screenwriter and make box office smash movies, or I would be a world-famous author with so many award-winning books to my name that it would make your head swim. In trying to choose between them, I realized it really didn't matter which of them I chose; I'd be world-famous regardless. In fact, I knew that if I became a writer, my novels would become so wildly popular that they'd be made *into* movies that I would one day direct—and star in—as well. I can still remember creating movies in my head as a kid. I'd define what the scenes would be and let them play out in my imagination—usually during school. Never mind the fact that I had no complete storylines; I had *ideas*. That was the fiery ember that never seemed to burn away.

By now, you're probably wondering, *Why in the world are you telling me this?* I tell you because it's important for you to understand why the chapters in this book are presented in the format they are. It all has to do with childhood dreams, right? I feel that it's important for you to remember this because of who I turned out to be when I got older.

You see, I became a teacher.

Yes, me. The boy who struggled in school for most of his childhood chose the pathway of educator. *But why?* I can almost hear you ask. *Why did you choose this career over those things you dreamed of doing when you were a kid?*

There are many answers to that question. There are so many influences that it would be hard for me to nail down one point of time as being the pivotal moment—the lynch pin, if you will—that decided the pathway to my career. While various teachers and life experiences were factors in my decision, it wasn't until I had graduated high school that my future as a teacher really began to shift into focus.

When I was a kid, becoming a teacher had never crossed my mind. I was going to be a rich and successful movie director/writer, remember? I'd be rubbing elbows and hobnobbing with the rich and famous amongst the glamor and glitz of a paparazzi-laden lifestyle. I was going to be *somebody*; I was not going to simply be a teacher.

Now, over a decade into my chosen profession, I am still not rubbing elbows with the rich—I am the bandager of elbows after war ball games. I don't hobnob at fancy restaurants with the elite—I eat lunch with ten-year-olds in a cafeteria. I don't meet with the scholars of the day—I am a molder of minds of those who are only just beginning to figure out who they really are. But you know what? I don't think I'd have it any other way. I guess the true reason I am a teacher is that I'm living my dream right now.

But wait, didn't you say that your dream was to become a movie director/actor/writer? How in the world does teaching factor into your dream?

Ah, such a good question.

You see, I *am* an actor. I am the masterful performer who stands before an audience of prepubescent little people that come to school at the beginning of the year either loving it, dreading it, or some point in between. My personal mission is to get each and every one of my students to love coming to school—the movie that I'm starring in. I try to make learning an enjoyable experience—an adventure—and when it comes time for them to leave after the end of 180 days together, they leave with a trove of knowledge they didn't have before.

I *am* a movie director, following the script which helps my students to define who it is they will be. I instill lessons of empathy and kindness daily, trying to get them to be the type of people who will effect society in a positive way.

I *am* a person who associates with the important people. When I head out with my students for a game of kickball, or sit with them in the overly-crowded cafeteria, they flock around me. I make them feel like they are the most important people in the world—because to me, they are.

I *do* write stories. These escapades materialize every single day in my classroom. They happen as an interaction between the students and the other important people in their lives. Sometimes these moments are humorous, at others times they may be deep and thoughtful, but whatever the interaction, these *are* the defining stories—the moments—of our lives.

I *am* living my childhood dream. However, so you truly understand this, I want to remind you of the boy I used to be (as well as the things teachers would write in my report cards). You see, it seems that every year in my class I have at least one student one who just can't keep still in his seat. He is a boy with ideas and dreams so big that it is nearly impossible for him to sit in that little, cramped desk for too long.

This kid might sound familiar to you.

I'd like you to meet 'Joey'. I'd like to share moments that he and I have come to experience together over the years. These are the scenes you will find on the following pages—moments in my teaching career—moments of a movie which has been playing for over a decade. These are just a few of the flashes through time that have made me laugh, cry, or simply shake my head and look on in amazement. These are the *Moments with Joey*. And though Joey's persona has been evidenced in a dozen different boys over the span of years, he is *that* boy...that one you remember from your own classroom. That kid who made you laugh during class, who talked to you when he wasn't supposed to, and—not trying to be a troublemaker—had just a little bit too much imagination for his own good.

My role has since changed. I am now at the other end of the classroom. I am the teacher responsible to guide him in his education for 180 days. I am the person who ignites the flame of learning so that it burns more fervently than it ever did before.

This is where my dream of being a screenwriter and movie director comes into play. This is why the stories on the ensuing pages are formatted as scripts. This just seemed to be the best way in which to portray these scenes through teaching. This is where my dream of being a screenwriter comes into the picture as well.

I'd now like to invite you in for a few glimpses of my world and some of the experiences Joey and I have shared together, in—and out—of the classroom; these stories through time that have come to be known as *Moments with Joey*.

"Cats. Mother Nature's way of saying: *Neener, neener…*"

— Melinda

<u>Joey Dosen't Like Kittys</u>

FADE IN:

INT. FIFTH GRADE CLASSROOM - MORNING

The teacher is giving a series of 5 different
spelling tests simultaneously to his class. He has
made it a point to use each student's name at least
once in a sentence. He has now reached the end,
having successfully used each student's name. There
are only a few words left on each list. The teacher
looks down at the current word: kitten. He pauses
momentarily, remembering a shirt he saw online a few
days before about grammar, and uses a similar
sentence.

                    TEACHER
          Kitten. Every time you spell one
          of your words incorrectly on this
          test, somewhere, a kitten dies.
          Kitten.

A ripple passes through the classroom, some students
are surprised, others are amused at the sentence
which was used.

CUT TO: A FEW MINUTES LATER.

The teacher is now checking over students' spelling
tests. Students hand the teacher their tests one at a
time. With each misspelled word, the teacher circles
the word and then hands the test back to the awaiting
student for them to make corrections. As he does
this, he makes comments to them.   ·

                    TEACHER
          Two wrong, Morgan? Bummer, it looks
          like you just killed two helpless little
          kittens. Better luck next time.

                    TEACHER
          Tanner, you only missed three this time!
          Great job; not too many kittens were
          sacrificed for your test today.

A boy, standing at the end of the line slowly makes

his way to the front. He is clutching his test to his chest like it is a letter from a dear friend. As it becomes his turn to get his test checked, he hands it over to the teacher. The teacher's eyes widen in surprise; Joey usually does far better than this.

>   TEACHER
> [hushed voice]
>   Joey, what happened? You usually
>   do much better than this on your
>   tests each week.

>   JOEY
> [Jokingly]
>   I don't like kittens.

The boy pauses, pretending to be in deep thought. After a moment he whispers:

>   How many kittens did we get
>   today?

>   TEACHER
> [Still caught off-guard]
>   Uh... about 26 altogether, I think.

Joey takes his test back and whispers in mock solemnness:

>   JOEY
>   Don't worry; I'll be able to get
>   a lot more of them *next* week.

Fade to black.

"I can't wait to grow up! Then I can say all the cuss words in the world."

—Crystal

Profanity

FADE IN:

INT. FIFTH GRADE CLASSROOM - LATE AFTERNOON

The school day has ended, and most of the students have gone home for the day. However, two boys remain, getting help on their variable homework from Math class at the back table. As one of the boys finishes up, his teacher requests his paper to check over the problems he's already done.

                    TEACHER
          So, did you work out these
          last few problems, Joey?

The teacher indicates several problems which are incorrect and have no work shown for them. The boy nods his head as he looks at the incorrectly-answered equations.

                    JOEY
          Um, yeah...

                    TEACHER
          Really? [Pause] You seemed to
          have missed quite a few of them...

Pause.

                    JOEY
          I did, Mr. Z, really. I swear.

                    TEACHER
          Really? I didn't think you did
          stuff like that.

The boy's face is blank for a second, and then takes on a look of shocked horror.

                    JOEY
          No, I mean, I worked the problems

20

                    out. I don't swear, I swear!

The boy stops in midsentence and covers his face with
his hands.

                         TEACHER

                Wait, so do you swear or don't
                you swear?

The boy looks up with a confused grin on his face.

                          JOEY
                No, I don't swear?

The teacher nods appreciatively and starts to look
over the boy's assignment once again.

                         TEACHER
                You promise?

                          JOEY
[The boy nods].
                Yeah, I swear.

Fade to black.

JOEY: I wear boxers.

TEACHER: Oh, so you're a fighter?

Super Atomic Wedges

FADE IN:

INT. LUNCHROOM - NOON

The teacher is eating lunch with his fifth-graders.
He listens to several conversations about who did
what over the weekend, who is who's latest crush, and
what the preferred after-school snack is, amongst
many other topics of conversation. The teacher is
tapped on the shoulder by the ten year-old boy
sitting next to him.

                    JOEY
          Hey, Mr. Z?

                    TEACHER
          What's up?

                    JOEY
          Have you ever gotten a wedgie
          before?

                    TEACHER
          A wedgie?

                    JOEY
          Yeah, it's when somebody grabs
          your underwear and pulls it up
          so that -

                    TEACHER
[Cutting him off]
          I know what a wedgie is, Joey.

                    JOEY
          So, have you ever had one before?

                    TEACHER
          Sorry to let you down... nope.

                    JOEY
          My favorite is the yo-yo wedgie.

                    TEACHER
          You have a favorite?

                         JOEY
               Yeah, there's the yo-yo wedgie,
               the chilly wedgie, the dangling
               wedgie...

                         TEACHER
               And you know about all of
               these different types?

                         JOEY
[Nodding].

               Yeah, but the yo-yo is my
               favorite; yo-yos are awesome.

                         TEACHER
               I don't know what to be more
               disturbed about...the fact that
               you know so many different
               types, or that you have a
               favorite one.

                         JOEY
               I got one once where I could
               almost taste it in my mouth...

                         TEACHER
               Sounds like a Super Atomic
               Wedgie.

                         JOEY
               Yeah, that's why I wear boxers
               now.

Fade to black.

"Wait Mom, you're the tooth fairy? Oh my gosh, does that mean Santa isn't real either?"

— Zander

Eye Doctors and Tooth Fairies

FADE IN:

INT. CLASSROOM - MORNING

The teacher is helping a young boy with his
equivalent fractions assignment before school. After
a few minutes, the boy starts to understand it, and
the teacher moves on to scoring journal entries.
After a several more minutes, the boy puts his pencil
down.

                    JOEY
          When I was little, I didn't
          believe in the eye doctor.
          [Pause]. But then I found out
          that he really does exist.

The teacher speaks offhandedly, not really paying
attention.

                    TEACHER
          Oh, so sort of like the
          opposite of the tooth fairy?

There is an intake of surprised breath from the boy,
and his eyes widen like fried eggs. The teacher
notices the look of shock on the boy's face and
quickly adds.

                    TEACHER
          Just kidding. The tooth fairy?
          Totally real.

The boy breathes out a sigh of relief and begins to
work on his assignment again.

                    JOEY
          I always knew it.

Fade to black.

"Sometimes I think about the fact that unicorns don't have hands, and it makes me sad. How do they play video games?"

— Miya

Vocabulary

FADE IN:

INT. CLASSROOM - AFTERNOON

The teacher moves to a desk where a young boy is
patiently waiting for help with his assignment. The
teacher kneels down next to him.

> JOEY
> Mr. Z, I was just doing the
> assignment and this question
> perplexed me.

The boy points to problem number four on his
worksheet while the teacher looks at the boy with a
surprised expression.

> TEACHER
> Perplexed? Do you even know
> what that word means?

> JOEY

[Nodding]
> Yeah, it means to be confused.

Pause.

> TEACHER
> How did you know that word, Joey?

> JOEY
> I don't know. [Shrug] I guess
> I'm just awesome.

> TEACHER
> Yeah, and it looks like you've
> got lots of humility, too.

The boy looks confused.

> JOEY
> What does "humility" mean?

Fade to black.

"Often I'm hilarious, but most of the time I'm just hysterical."

— Tami

Tracking Hilarity

FADE IN:

INT. CLASSROOM - MORNING

The teacher is taking roll for the day and submitting attendance to the office. As he does, he notices one of his fifth-grade students standing in front of him with a blue sticky note and a pen. The boy is smiling as wide as Christmas.

                    TEACHER:
          Yes?

The boy smiles even wider and rocks forward on his toes.

                    JOEY
          You're a funny guy. Did you
          know that?

                    TEACHER
          Yeah, I'm pretty much fraught
          with hilarity.

                    JOEY
          See, there you go again. You're
          always making us laugh with
          jokes and stuff. It makes the day
          go quicker and it's a lot of fun.

                    TEACHER
          I guess it helps that you can't
          laugh and throw up at the same time.

                    JOEY
          There's another one!

                    TEACHER
          Another one what?

                    JOEY
          Something funny.

There is a pause while the boy puts two tally marks

on the sticky note.

                    JOEY
          You know what I'm going to do?
          I'm going to keep track of
          every time you say something
          funny all day on this piece
          of paper. At the end of the
          day, I'll know just how funny
          you really are.

                    TEACHER
          Wow, my own personal funniness
          meter! You know, I might just
          have to scrape the rust off of
          my personality for today.

                    JOEY
          That was funny, too.

The boy adds another tally to the note and returns to
his desk, looking expectantly at the teacher.

CUT TO INTERIOR CLASSROOM SHOTS. MIDMORNING THROUGH
AFTERNOON.

Various quick cuts of the teacher as he is giving
instructions and interacting with his students
throughout the day. These shots are interspersed
throughout a variety of lessons. Quick shots are also
of Joey as the boy 'rates' his teacher discretely
with either a thumbs up, down, or a shake of the hand
indicating the level to which he is impressed by the
comments throughout the day. Tally marks are made on
the sticky note during this time. A song plays in the
background during the medley of clips: 'You're the
Best' by Joe Esposito, originally used in the movie,
The Karate Kid.

                    TEACHER
          You are not only the student,
          but also the pet I never had
          but always wanted. [Thumbs up]

                    TEACHER
          You do realize that if you have
          an accident, you're going to

31

have to clean it up yourself.
[Thumbs up].

                    TEACHER
The answer to the math problem
can never be bacon. It's delicious,
but it's never the answer.
[Thumbs up].

                    TEACHER
I guess if you were drowning
you could always stand on your
head and you'd be safe, right?
[Wavered hand].

                    TEACHER
If your head explodes, I'll
just put it in a plastic baggie
and give it to your mom after
school. [Thumbs up].

                    TEACHER
I'm not sure if I have a soul,
I never checked. [Thumbs up].

                    TEACHER
Look; if you don't go out
to recess, then I can't
start missing you now can
I? [Thumbs up].

Spoken to three dawdling boys as the class is lining
up to go to lunch.

                    TEACHER
Mimsy, Muffy, Buffy, let's
get a move on here... I'm not
getting any younger and neither
are the three of you. But I am
getting better looking every.
single. minute. Pretty soon I'm
going to start blinding you all
with my good looks. [Thumbs up].

                    TEACHER

32

If my darkest nightmares had
a soundtrack and choreography,
I think it would look and sound
something just like this. [Thumbs up].

                    TEACHER
The book usually works a whole
lot better if you open it first.
[Wavered hand].

                    TEACHER
You do realize that you're
breathing my air, don't you?
[Thumbs up].

                    TEACHER
Be careful when reaching in
your desk, Joey pulled a pony
out of his yesterday. It was in
the back, stuffed behind an
old bologna sandwich. [Thumbs up].

                    TEACHER
[Spoken to a boy].
          Okay Buttercream, let's get to
          work while we're still all
          capable of breathing. [Thumbs up].

CUT TO:

INT. CLASSROOM - AFTERNOON

The bell has just sounded; the students are giving
the teacher high-fives and a few are giving him a
quick hug as they depart the classroom. One boy holds
back as he counts the tallies from his sticky note.
After a minute he writes a number on the paper that
he circles; he approaches the teacher.

                    JOEY
          Mr. Z, you were pretty funny
          today.

The boy taps the sticky note with the pen he's been
using.

                    TEACHER

Really? So I made the cut?

                    JOEY
          Well, there *were* some lame
          things you said today, but
          I didn't keep track of those.

                    TEACHER
          Thank heaven for small miracles
          and slatherings of awesomeness.

The boy starts to laugh and makes another tally mark
on his sticky note.

                    JOEY
          Mr. Z, you were funny a total
          of 86 times today-that's *really*
          funny!

Pause.

                    TEACHER
          That's probably why they pay me
          the big bucks.

There is a pause as the boy stares bemusedly at the
teacher for a moment.

                    TEACHER
          Um... that was a joke.

                    JOEY
          Yeah, but it wasn't very funny.

                    TEACHER
          You're telling me...

Fade to black.

"On days when I'm sad, I look into the mirror and lovingly remind myself that there's no shame in occasionally feeling like a trash goblin."

— Miya

<u>Daylight Saving</u>

FADE IN:

INT. CLASSROOM - AFTERNOON

The teacher is working with a small group of kids on
math skills. The four kids are clustered at the back
table. One boy motions to the watch he's wearing.

                    JOEY
          Mr. Z, did you see my watch?

                    TEACHER
          Wow, is it new?

The boy grins, shakes his head, and heads back to the
table.

                    JOEY
          Nope, but the last time I wore it
          was about sixth months ago.

                    TEACHER
[Unbelievingly]
          Six *months*?

                    JOEY
          Yeah, I don't know how to change
          the time on it.

Pause.

                    TEACHER
          And let me guess, Daylight
          Saving Time?

The boy looks sheepish.

                    JOEY
          Yeah, I guess I haven't worn
          it for a while.

                    TEACHER
          Well, enjoy it for the next
          six months.

Fade to black.

"I'm a pretty good-lookin' little boy; that's why all the girls chase me during recess."

— Isaac

<u>Hot, Hotter, and Hottest</u>

FADE IN:

INT. FIFTH GRADE CLASSROOM - AFTERNOON

The teacher is helping a few fifth-grade students at
the back table on a math assignment during recess.
The classroom is somewhat toasty, and the teacher has
opened the door and set up the fan to blow in some
cool air.

                    JOEY:
          I'm hot, Mr. Z.

                    TEACHER
          Oh really?

The boy thinks for a second.

                    JOEY
          Yeah, hot *both* ways... if
          you know what I mean!

                    TEACHER
          Thanks for the news flash.

Pause.

                    JOEY
          So my mom's checking me out...

                    TEACHER
          Really? Your mom is *checking
          you out?*

The boy pauses for a split second before looking
aghast.

                    JOEY
          No! I mean she's going to be
          checking me out of school early.
          Not *checking me out.*

                    TEACHER

> That's a relief. Otherwise that
> would be weird.

The boy giggles and then starts working. After a
minute he looks back up at his teacher.

> JOEY
> I'm hot.

> TEACHER
> I know, I've got the *same* problem.

Fade to black.

"If dreams really can come true, what does that say about our nightmares?"

— Shawna

<u>Dreams and Nightmares</u>

FADE IN:

INT. CLASSROOM - MORNING

The class is taking their seats before the tardy bell
rings and announcements start. As the teacher begins
to take attendance, a fifth-grade boy approaches him
and whispers quietly.

> JOEY
> I had a dream about you last
> night.

> TEACHER
> You realize that I don't
> normally make home visits
> during the school year,
> don't you?

The boy grins.

> JOEY
> You were chasing me.

Pause.

> TEACHER
> Well, lots of people have
> dreams with other people in them.

> JOEY
> But did you know that there's
> a lot of kids that have dreams
> about you where they're hurt,
> stressed out, or that you're
> chasing after them?

Pause.

> TEACHER
> And just what was your dream
> about? *Why* was I chasing you?

> JOEY

You were trying to sell me on
the Internet...

                    TEACHER
          I was trying to *sell* you?

                    JOEY
          Yeah, it was a nightmare.

                    TEACHER
          Well, one boy's nightmare
          is another teacher's dream.

Pause.

                    JOEY
          So, you dream about me, huh?

Fade to black.

"When my sister says she'll be out of the bathroom in a minute, it's more like an hour. When I'm in the bathroom and say I'll be out in a minute, it really is a minute... unless I'm trying to make her mad."

— Tyler

Resting Rooms

FADE IN:

INT. CLASSROOM - MIDMORNING

The class is working in small groups on math review
problems as the teacher moves from group to group,
checking over their work. As he moves across the room
he is approached by a fifth-grade boy.

>   JOEY
>   Mr. Z, I'm going to the rest
>   room, okay?

>   TEACHER
>   Oh, are you tired?

The boy looks confused before an expression of
dawning comprehension flashes across his face.

>   JOEY
>   What I meant is that I'm going
>   to go to the bathroom.

>   TEACHER
>   You're going to take a bath?
>   Here at school?

The boy shakes his head and tries to hide a smile. He
rolls his eyes and tries to use a sarcastic tone.

>   JOEY
>   Yeah, I thought I'd take one
>   in the toilet.

Pause.

>   TEACHER
>   Well, you better flush twice
>   then...

The boy chokes on a laugh as he picks up the
basketball hall pass filled with rocks and moves out
into the hallway.

Fade to black.

<u>Can I?</u>

FADE IN:

INT. CLASSROOM - MORNING

The students are completing an assignment on the Promethean board. One student punctuates a portion of the incorrect sentence and then passes on the pen to another child to fix something else. The teacher is observing from the reading table as he is approached by a fifth-grade boy.

                    JOEY
          Hey, Mr. Z?

                    TEACHER
          What, Joey?

The boy leans in a little bit.

                    JOEY
          Can I go to the bathroom?

The teacher shakes his head as he looks at the boy—he recalls the incorrect usage of this particular word – the same mistake he used to make all the time as a kid and recollects the response HIS teachers always gave to him.

                    TEACHER
          I don't know, Joey, *can* you?

The boy looks at the teacher, unfazed.

                    JOEY
          Yeah, I can prove it; you wanna see?

                    TEACHER
[Surprised]
          Uh, no, not really.

Pause.

                    JOEY
          So, can I go?

                    TEACHER
          Yeah, I guess you can…

Fade to black.

"Sometimes I can't sleep because my brain is full of thinking."

— Nathan

Deep Thoughts

FADE IN:

INT. LUNCHROOM - NOON

The teacher has just finished his lunch. He rises
from the table of fifth-graders and begins to walk
back toward the classroom. As he walks down the
hallway, a boy materializes at his side. For a
second, neither of them speak.

                    JOEY
          Mr. Z, what are you thinking about?

The teacher looks at the boy with a shrug.

                    TEACHER
          I don't know, why?

The boy lays a hand on the teacher's arm.

                    JOEY
          Think *hard* about that, Mr. Z.

                    TEACHER
          About what?

[The boy rolls his eyes].

                    JOEY
          Keep thinking hard about *that*...
          keep thinking... Mr. Z? Are you
          still thinking? Keep thinking
          about that. Thinking, thinking,
          always thinking. Keep on thinking
          about that...

                    TEACHER
          Do you know what, Joey? It just
          so happens that I AM thinking
          about something... like putting
          you into a wooden box, nailing
          it shut, and dropping it in the
          middle of the lake.

The boy stops in his tracks for a second and then falls back in step with his teacher.

                    JOEY
          Stop thinking... stop thinking...
          don't think too hard about that...

Fade to black.

"Sometimes I wish people had a minimize button so I could click it and make them go away."

— Herbie

<u>Annoying and Distracting</u>

FADE IN:

INT. CLASSROOM - LATE AFTERNOON

The teacher is working with two students who've
stayed after school to complete homework assignments.
Becky is using a set of colored pencils to finish up
her vocabulary poster. As she colors, she pauses to
shake her hand as it's become 'tired'. After a few
moments, the boy looks up from his spelling
assignment and fixes her with a look.

                    JOEY
          Would you please quit doing
          that? It's annoying AND
          distracting.

Becky pauses for a moment and then starts up again.

                    BECKY
          I could, but my hand is tired
          and this helps it to feel better.

The boy rolls his eyes and turns in his desk so as
not to have her in his sights as he continues on his
homework. In a few moments, Becky has finished. She
gathers up her books and leaves for the day. Joey and
the teacher sit in silence for a few moments when
Joey starts to flap both of his hands; the teacher
ignores this at first, but then it becomes quite
annoying AND distracting.

                    TEACHER
          Joey, just what are you doing?
          You look like the winner of a
          Miss America Pageant.

The boy lets loose a giggle as he flaps his hands
even harder.

                    JOEY
          It looks like I'm drying my
          nails, doesn't it?

                    TEACHER
          Actually, you look like some
          type of freaky cheerleader.

The boy continues to flap both of his hands.

                    TEACHER
          Joey, I thought you said that
          that was annoying.

                    JOEY
          It is. [Pause]. But I never
          knew just how fun it was before.

                    TEACHER
          Even if it's annoying for
          everybody else?

                    JOEY
          No, *because* it is...

Fade to black.

"Breakfast is not meant to be eaten slow, otherwise they would call it breakslow."

—Brent

Life and Milk Cartons

FADE IN:

EXT. BLACKTOP - MORNING

The class is lined up and readying themselves to come into the building. As the class president picks the straighter of the two lines, the students file past the teacher with a flurry of 'Good mornings' and greetings of 'Hello, Mr. Z.' The teacher acknowledges each of his students as they pass by. Toward the end of the line a fifth-grade boy walks up slowly, he is clutching his stomach.

> JOEY
> [Spoken as if he's sick].
> Ugh, Mr. Z... I am *SC* stuffed.

The teacher and boy walk through the set of double doors together and start down the hallway behind the rest of the class.

> TEACHER
> Why, what happened?

The boy grins.

> JOEY
> I had two breakfasts this morning.

> TEACHER
> *Two* breakfasts?

> JOEY
> Yeah, down in the lunchroom I had two orders of French toast, two orders of sausage, two servings of fruit, two bowls of cereal, and two cartons of milk. [Pause]. I went though the line twice.

> TEACHER
> Holy Hannah, Joey, why did you eat so much?

                    JOEY
          Well, they say breakfast *is*
          the most important meal of
          the day, Mr. Z.

                    TEACHER
          So, I guess I can expect twice
          as much out of you today then,
          right?

Pause.

                    JOEY
          Yep... and you know what?

                    TEACHER
          What's that?

                    JOEY
          Some people think I should have
          my picture on a box of Life cereal
          because I'm good-looking, too.

                    TEACHER
          Well, it beats having it on
          a milk carton.

Fade to black.

"We were out playing on the monkey bars during recess and Robert had a bee fly into his shirt. He just hung there crying because he thought it was going to sting him. I guess the bee didn't want him to feel sad, so it did."

— Caden

The Wasp
FADE IN:

INT. CLASSROOM - AFTERNOON

Several students remain in the classroom working on
missing homework assignments. The teacher is helping
a young boy on a math worksheet. After working a few
problems with the teacher, the boy looks up.

                    JOEY
          Mr. Z?

                    TEACHER
          What's up, Joey?

                    JOEY
          I got stung by a wasp...
          seventeen times.

                    TEACHER
          Seventeen times?

The boy nods and sets his pencil down.

                    JOEY
          Yep. He stung me here
          [points to back], here
          [points to neck], here
          [points to arms], and here
          [points to chest].

                    TEACHER
          Wow, I'm just amazed that you
          stood there and let it sting
          you that many times. That's
          probably not the smartest thing
          you've ever done.

                    JOEY
          No, I didn't just stand there,
          I was running away, but he
          chased me and kept stinging me...
          seventeen times!

                    TEACHER
          Seventeen times? Maybe there
          was more than one wasp; maybe
          he was attacking you with his
          wasp gang.

The boy shakes his head adamantly.

                    JOEY
          Nope, he was the only one.

                    TEACHER
          What did you do to make him mad?
          Make fun of his mom?

The boy gives a sorrowful nod and fakes Bambi eyes.

                    TEACHER
          Well, *that* explains everything.
          You totally got what you deserved.
          If I were a wasp and you made fun
          of *my* mom, I'd have stung you, too.

                    JOEY
          Seventeen times?

                    TEACHER
          Eighteen.

Fade to black.

"I wish people would pay me money instead of compliments."

— Kobe

The Dime

FADE IN:

EXT. PLAYGROUND - AFTERNOON

The teacher is on recess duty and is supervising the
fifth and sixth graders as they play wall ball,
kickball, and the other various games taking place.
As he is walking along the blacktop, a fifth-grade
boy approaches him.

                    JOEY
          Mr. Z, guess what?

                    TEACHER
          You got beat up by a bunch of
          kindergarten girls again?

                    JOEY
          Yeah, that too, but this is
          something else.

                    TEACHER
          Fire away.

The boy looks around to make sure that he isn't being
overheard, and then leans in close.

                    JOEY
          I swallowed a dime last week.

                    TEACHER
          Oh. So, were you trying to...
          change?

The teacher starts to laugh. The boy ignores him and
continues.

                    JOEY
          I was just throwing it up in
          the air and catching it in my
          mouth when, GULP! Down it went!

                    TEACHER
          Bummer, now you're ten cents
          poorer than you were before.

                    JOEY
          Well, you know I can always
          look for it when it comes out
          later.

Pause.

                    TEACHER
          Okay, now that's just gross,
          Joey.

                    JOEY
          But you know what, Mr. Z? I
          hope it *never* comes out, that
          way I'll always be worth ten
          cents!

                    TEACHER
          You know what, Joey? You're worth
          a heck of a lot more than ten
          cents.

Fade to black.

"Mom, why doesn't our house ever get stealed or catch on fire? Our family is so boring!"

— Herbie

Ententertainment Starved
FADE IN:

INT. CLASSROOM - AFTERNOON

The teacher is out on recess duty. He is walking
around the playground when one of his students comes
running up. The boy falls in step with the teacher
and is silent for several moments. The boy stares at
the teacher's forearm which is showing from
underneath his rolled up sleeves. The boy looks down
at his own arm, and then back at the teacher's. After
a minute, the boy holds his own arm up.

                    JOEY
          Mr. Z, did you know that I
          have almost as much arm hair
          as you do?

                    TEACHER
          Not quite, Joey. I'm afraid
          you're going to have to wait
          until you go through puberty.

                    JOEY
[Confused]
          Puberty?

                    TEACHER
          Yeah, you know. When you start
          to get hair under your arms.

The boy's face breaks into an excited grin as he
points to both his left and right armpits.

                    JOEY
          I've already got eight of them!
          I've got five under this arm
          and three under this one![Pause]
          I haven't named them yet...

                    TEACHER
          Wow, I'll bet your parents are
          proud of you.

                    JOEY
[Brightly]

64

> They are. It was kind of a
> big deal at my house, you know.

                    TEACHER
[Surprised]

> Really? Because it sounds more
> like you're kind of starved for
> entertainment.

The boy nods and a solemn look flashes across his
face.

                    JOEY
> Yeah, tell me about it.

Fade to black.

"I do not have mom's genes, they're way too big for me."

— Matthew

Genes and Brains

FADE IN:

INT. CLASSROOM - AFTERNOON

The class has just completed a lesson on heredity.
They've put away their Science notebooks and are
heading out to recess. One boy lingers behind the
others. When the room clears, he approaches his
teacher.

                    JOEY
          Mr. Z, is it really true?

                    TEACHER
          Is what really true?

                    JOEY
          That our genes really decide
          who we are? You know, our hair
          color, how tall we are, and all
          that stuff?

                    TEACHER
          Yep. There were about 70 trillion
          different ways you could have
          turned out.

Pause.

                    JOEY
          I think I got ripped off...

The teacher stares at the boy for a second.

                    TEACHER
          Ripped off? Now why on earth
          would you say that?

                    JOEY
[Whispered]
          I don't think I got a brain.

The teacher grins.

                    TEACHER
          Well, you know what? I hear
          that brains are overrated anyhow.
          You probably don't really even need
          one.

Pause.

                    JOEY
          Well, I still think I got ripped
          off. [Pause]. Hey, there's always
          brain transplants, right? Maybe I
          could get yours!

                    TEACHER
          And take the risk of you learning
          all my teacher secrets? I don't
          think so.

                    JOEY
          Now THAT would be awesome.

                    TEACHER
          Get used to rip-offs...

Fade to black.

"I always tell people that I'm not a cat person or a dog person; frankly, I'm barely a people person."

— Tonya

The Pet

FADE IN:

INT. CLASSROOM - MORNING

The students are leaving the classroom for afternoon
recess. The teacher takes a few books which need
shelving and heads to the bookshelf in the corner of
the room; he is stopped by a boy still sitting at his
desk by that corner.

                    JOEY
          Mr. Z?

                    TEACHER
          What's up, Joey?

                    JOEY
          I was just wondering...
          what if I was a cat?

                    TEACHER
[Confused]
          A cat?

The boy nods his head and then grins at the teacher.

                    JOEY
          Yeah, but not just *any* cat...
          your cat.

The teacher looks at the boy for a moment then shakes
his head.
                    TEACHER
          I'm afraid that I'd have to
          get rid of you. You see, I'm
          allergic to cats.

The boy sits for a second with a furrowed brow and
then looks at the teacher again with shining eyes.

                    JOEY
What if I was a dog?

                    TEACHER
I don't think so, dogs really
belong outside. Besides, my yard
isn't really big enough for a dog.
I'd have to get rid of you.

                    JOEY
A talking bird?

                    TEACHER
Talking birds are annoying.
Sorry, I can't stand them.

                    JOEY
A monkey?

                    TEACHER
I really don't have a place to
keep a monkey, and they're not my
favorite animal anyway. I'm afraid
you'd have to go.

                    JOEY
What if I was a small pet? Would
you keep me?

                    TEACHER
Animals really aren't my style,
Joey. Sorry.

                    JOEY
What about a fifth-grader?

                    TEACHER
Now *that* I'd keep.

Fade to black.

"Mom, does my breath smell kinda like poop to you?"

— Claire

<u>Inappropriateness</u>
FADE IN:

INT. FIFTH GRADE CLASSROOM - MORNING

The teacher is standing at the front of the class; he is pointing out a series of vocabulary words written on the dry erase board. Students are giving the definition and are using the said words correctly in either an example or sentence.

> TEACHER
> Now, whose word is 'rallied'?

A hand shoots in the air. The teacher indicates the student who promptly replies:

> STUDENT 1
> It means to come together
> as a group.

> TEACHER
> Excellent! Would you please
> give me an example using your
> word?

Student thinks for a moment before answering.

> STUDENT 1
> The class rallied together
> at the assembly in the gym.

> TEACHER
> Fantastic! Whose word is this?

Teacher points at the word 'deadline'. Another student raises her hand and responds with the correct definition.

> TEACHER
> Would you please give me an
> example of 'deadline'?

> STUDENT 1
> Our literature responses are
> due on Monday; that's the
> deadline.

74

                              TEACHER
              Wonderful!

The teacher points to one of the final words on the
board. The word is 'inappropriate.' A boy's hand
punches the air.

                         TEACHER
              Would you please tell me the
              definition of the word,
              'inappropriate'?

                         JOEY
              To do something not socially
              acceptable for where you are.

                         TEACHER
              Would you please give me an
              example of 'inappropriate'?

Joey pauses, thinking.

                         JOEY
              Yeah, pooping in your pants
              during class.

General laughter percolates the classroom as the
teacher stands, speechless. He nervously glances
about the room, unsure of just how to proceed at this
point. After an uncomfortable beat he continues.

                         TEACHER
              Right, Joey. That *would* be
              inappropriate.

                         JOEY
[Spoken quietly]
              That's why *I'll* never do it.

Fade to black.

"There's something amazing about driving down the road with the windows open and blasting your favorite music; however, Barry Manilow doesn't quite cut it."

— Jason

Music

FADE IN:

INT. FIFTH GRADE CLASSROOM - MORNING

Class is in session, and one student, 'Becky,' has
just completed a literature response by playing a
song. The teacher starts to address the class as the
last few strains of the song fade.

                    TEACHER
          Music is powerful. It has a
          way of opening up a conduit—
          or pathway—of time, allowing
          a person to remember memories
          from when they first heard it.

                    BOY 1:
          Like when a song is used in a movie?

TEACHER

          Exactly. The next time you hear
          that song, what do you think of?

                    CLASS
[In unison]
          The movie.

                    TEACHER
          That's right, because music can
          speak to us in a way that not
          many other things can. When a
          character in a book loves a
          particular song, we will often
          associate that song with the
          character.

                    BOY 2
          Like in the book, The Watsons
          go to Birmingham—1963?

                    TEACHER
          Exactly! In the story, what
          is Kenny's favorite song?

                    BOY 2
          "Yakkity-Yak."

                    TEACHER
          And what do *you* think of when
          you hear that song?

                    BOY 2
          Kenny.

                    TEACHER
          Music can do that for us. In
          fact one day you'll be sitting
          in your car, your own kids
          will be screaming in the backseat,
          and as you fumble with the radio
          you'll come across a station
          playing "Don't Stop" by Fleetwood
          Mac. Even as you sit there,
          you'll be transported back
          through the years. You'll find
          yourself sitting in this classroom
          for just a brief second; you'll
          see all of us gathered together
          singing to the guitar. It's at
          that point that you'll start to
          wonder, 'Did Lance become a
          lawyer after all?' 'Did Bree
          and Andrew get married?' You'll
          even wonder, 'Hey, is Mr. Z even
          still alive anymore?'

                    JOEY
          And is he still as good-looking
          as back when he was my teacher?

The class bursts into laughter. The teacher, not
having lost composure, brings the class back to order
and then turns to face Joey.

                    TEACHER
          We can only hope...

Fade to black.

"The greatest gift I could ever receive for Teacher Appreciation Week would be for all the sixth-graders to wear deodorant for an entire week straight."

— Abe

Hard Work and Good Smells

FADE IN:

INT. SCHOOL LIBRARY - AFTERNOON

Most of the class is in the kiva, practicing a rap
song about the presidents of the United States to a
karaoke track of Coolio's "Gangster's Paradise." As
the teacher checks on the four or five students
working on their homework in the library, one boy
approaches him.

                    JOEY

          Mr. Z, I only have one assignment
          left and then I'm all caught up!

                    TEACHER
          Joey, I'm so proud of you; you've
          worked awfully hard.

The boy stands there for a second and then throws his
arms around his teacher, giving him a huge hug. With
his face buried in his teacher's shirt, the boy takes
a deep breath.
                    JOEY
          It's all because of you, Mr. Z...
          you...[pause] Man, you smell
          SC good!

Pause.

                    TEACHER
          You know, I don't know whether I
          should be flattered or just
          creeped out.

The boy releases his teacher and grins.

                    JOEY
          Old Spice?

                    TEACHER
          Okay, I'm creeped out.

                    JOEY
          You're welcome, Mr. Z...

Fade to black.

Dreams and Nightmares #2

FADE IN:

INT. HALLWAY - AFTERNOON

The class is taking a 3-minute break. A few of the kids are lined up and ready to return to the classroom. As the teacher waits at the front, facing the lines, a fifth-grade boy moves out of line and approaches the teacher.

                    JOEY
          I had a dream last night, Mr. Z.

                    TEACHER
          I used to have dreams, too; most
          of them withered and died.

The boy give the teacher a 'yeah, right' look.

                    JOEY
          No, I had a *real* dream.

                    TEACHER
          Yeah, me too.

                    JOEY
          Really?

                    TEACHER
          Don't you remember? You were
          there. [When the boy doesn't answer,
          the teacher continues]. You were
          riding on a unicorn through outer
          space. [Pause] I don't know how on
          earth you were both able to breathe
          out there.

                    JOEY
          So... it was a good dream?

                    TEACHER
          Nope, that's the point when it
          pretty much became a nightmare.

The boy starts laughing with the rest of the class.

Fade to black.

"I usually judge someone's character by the number of friends they have on Facebook."

— George

Popularity

FADE IN:

INT. CAFETERIA – NOONISH

The students are passing through the lunch line, and
the teacher stands by, making sure that they enter
their lunch numbers correctly (as well as have at
least three items on their trays). After some
deliberation, he decides to get school lunch as well—
after all, the aroma of potatoes and gravy is nearly
overwhelming. The teacher slips into line and fills
his tray, then scans the lunchroom for a place to
sit.

The table he usually sits at on the days he eats in
the lunchroom has only three **fifth-grade** students
sitting at it. The teacher moves to the table and
sits down. Like magic, the three boys at the table
scoot over to where the teacher is, and nine or ten
students from other tables battle for positions on
the benches as well. As the commotion dies down and
the students begin eating, the fifth-grade boy
sitting next to the teacher pauses and looks at him.

>   JOEY
>   Did you see that, Mr. Z?

>   TEACHER
>   See what?

>   JOEY
>   This table was practically
>   empty, and then suddenly—boom!
>   It's overcrowded. Some people
>   didn't even have a space to sit.

>   TEACHER
>   Yeah, it seems a bit full doesn't
>   it?

Pause.

>   JOEY
>   I just can't believe how *popular*
>   I am.

The teacher smiles as he takes a drink of his milk.

                    TEACHER
          It's probably because you
          wore deodorant today.

                    JOEY
          Yeah, I should do that more
          often.

                    TEACHER
          Well, I sure know that *I'd*
          appreciate it.

Fade to black.

"Sometimes I wish I had a unicorn. Not because it could fly or grant wishes, but because he could use his horn to get even with all the bullies who've picked on me."

— William

<u>Unicorn Lockdown</u>

FADE IN:

INT. HALLWAY - NOON

The school has just been removed from lockdown
status. The students are taking the rest of their
lunch recess indoors. The teacher is returning to the
classroom from the cafeteria with one of his fifth-
grade students. After a few moments, the boy turns to
his teacher.

                    JOEY
          Why was the school on lockdown,
          Mr. Z?

                    TEACHER
          We already talked about the
          reasons a school would go on
          lockdown in class, Joey; it was
          probably nothing.

                    JOEY
          So, was there anyone dangerous
          here at the school?

                    TEACHER
          Just because a school goes on
          lockdown doesn't mean that there's
          dangerous men in masks running
          around in the hallways.

                    JOEY
          Really?

                    TEACHER
          I'm serious, Joey... everything's
          fine.

The boy flashes the teacher a serious look

                    JOEY
          Mr. Z...

The teacher pauses in the hallway and faces the boy.
He looks to the left and right before speaking in a

low, conspiratorial voice.

> TEACHER
> Okay, here's the real story...
> the one you're not supposed to
> know about.

The teacher pauses, and the boy leans in slightly.

> TEACHER (CONT.)
> A unicorn was sighted out on the
> playground. *[The boy raises an
> eyebrow]*. The principal called
> for a lockdown because it was
> prancing back and forth, shooting
> magical rainbow wishes from its
> mane and tail; you see, he didn't
> want to share any of the wishes
> with the rest of the school, he
> wanted to keep them all to himself.

The boy tries not to smile and rolls his eyes.

> JOEY
> Sure, Mr. Z...

> TEACHER
> Hey... for unicorn wishes, I'd
> have called for a lockdown, too.

CUT TO:

INT. HALLWAY - NOON

Lunch recess has ended and the teacher is reminding
the students a second time of proper procedure during
a lockdown. After a few moments one of the students
raises his hand.

> TEACHER
> What's your question, Joey?

> JOEY
> What if somebody breaks into
> our classroom?

                    TEACHER
          Then I'd have to protect you all
          with my ninja skills and sheer
          awesomeness.

A ripple of laughter moves through the class.

                    JOEY
          What if he were really tough
          though?

                    TEACHER
          Then I'm afraid I'd have to
          use *these*...

The teacher holds up his fists with a flourish and
grins.

                    TEACHER (CONT.)
          In fact, if I were to put them
          into my pockets, I'd probably
          be arrested for carrying concealed
          weapons.

The class bursts into laughter.

Fade to black.

<u>Hotness</u>

FADE IN:

INT. FIFTH GRADE CLASSROOM - AFTERNOON.

The teacher is entering grades during lunch recess.
As he works, he is approached by a fifth-grade boy
who really should be working on missing assignments.

> JOEY
> I'm ten.

> TEACHER
> That's great Joey. Did you
> need anything?

The boy thinks for a second.

> JOEY
> Nope. I'm ten.

> TEACHER
> Yeah, I used to be ten once,
> Too... I used to be little and
> cute, and then I got big and
> ugly.

> JOEY
> Like me?

> TEACHER
> You're big and ugly?

> JOEY
> No, Mr. Z. I'm hot!

The boy stands for a second before breaking into
song.

> JOEY
> ♫♪ Don't cha wish ♪ yo teacha
> was hot like me ♫....

> TEACHER
> Yeah, I used to think I was
> funny once, too...

Fade to black.

"Whenever I'm home, my brothers and I fight a lot. When I go away to camp or a sleepover, and nobody's there for them to fight with, they miss me."

— Mark

Camping Trips

FADE IN:

INT. CLASSROOM - AFTERNOON

The teacher is working with a small group of students during recess. They are all seated at the kidney-shaped table at the back of the classroom. After working for several minutes, one boy looks up from his assignment.

                    JOEY
          Mr. Z, have you ever gone
          camping before?

                    TEACHER
          Yeah.

An impressed expression flashes across the boy's face.

                    JOEY
          Probably like a hundred times,
          right?

                    TEACHER
          Well, I've gone quite a bit.

The boy slouches in his chair for a moment.

                    JOEY
          I've only gone camping once,
          and that was in the backyard.

Pause.

                    JOEY
          Hey, maybe *you* could take me
          camping, Mr. Z!

                    TEACHER
          Me?

                    JOEY
          Yeah, like on Survivor Man.

Pause.

                    TEACHER
          If we went camping like on
          Survivor Man, we'd both head
          out to the desert, but only
          one of us would come back...
          I'd probably have to use you
          as firewood.

There is a long pause and then the boy continues to
work on his assignment.

                    JOEY
          I've heard that camping is lame.

                    TEACHER
          It probably is...

Fade to black.

"The thing that I don't like most about my school is that it isn't Hogwarts."

— Randy

Too Many Jokers, Not Enough Aces

FADE IN:

INT. CLASSROOM - AFTERNOON

The rain is pelting down from the sky outside and can
be heard plainly on the roof. The students are taking
part in various inside activities as the teacher
enters the math scores for the day. He becomes
conscious of one fifth-grade boy who utters numbers
repeatedly, like Dustin Hoffman from Rain Man.

                    JOEY
[From across the room, muttered]
          42..52..42..42..52 [Louder]
          Mr. Z, 42!

The teacher looks up from his laptop.

                    TEACHER
          Joey, what in the world are
          you talking about?

The boy holds up a handful of playing cards.

                    JOEY
          I only have 42 cards!

                    TEACHER
          And what does that mean?

The boy pauses for a second.

                    JOEY
          I'm not playing with a full deck?

                    TEACHER
          You said it, not me...

The boy bursts out laughing.

Fade to black.

Transformations

FADE IN:

INT. CLASSROOM - MORNING

The class is taking their seats before the tardy bell
rings. A fifth-grade boy digs a set of papers from
his backpack and brings these to his teacher, giving
his head a shake, flipping the hair hanging in his
eyes to one side.

                    JOEY
          Mr. Z, can I turn these
          forms into the office?

The teacher feigns a look of shocked surprise.

                    TEACHER
          Whoa, Joey, how in the world
          are you **going** to do that? With
          a magic wand? This isn't Hogwarts,
          you know...

The boy looks confused for a moment before rephrasing
his statement with another flip of his overgrown
hair.

                    JOEY
          May I give these forms to the
          office?

                    TEACHER
          Yeah, I suppose you should.

                    JOEY
          Thanks Mr. Z.

                    TEACHER
          Anytime there, Hagrid.

Pause.

                    JOEY
          Yeah, I need a haircut, too...

Fade to black.

"If you're driving your mom crazy and she yells, 'Do I look like an idiot?' Don't answer her, it's a trap."

— Louis

<u>License to Drive</u>

FADE IN:

INT. CLASSROOM - LATE AFTERNOON

The class has left for the day; the teacher is
packing up his items to go. As he slides his computer
into the case, a fifth-grade boy 'drives' around the
classroom on the teacher's wheeled chair. He is
making 'vrooming' noises as he does so.

                    JOEY
          Are you driving home tonight,
          Mr. Z?

                    TEACHER
          Yep.

                    JOEY
          You know, if you wanted, I could
          drive you...

                    TEACHER
          Wouldn't you need a license to
          drive, Joey?

The boy grins.
                    JOEY
          Oh, I've got a license, Mr. Z.

                    TEACHER
          Really?

                    JOEY
          Yep, I got it when I was ten.

                    TEACHER
          A license for what?

                    JOEY
          Driving you crazy.

Pause.
                    TEACHER
          Yeah, isn't *that* the truth.

Fade to black.

Geysers and Boysers

FADE IN:

INT. HALLWAY - MORNING

The students are taking a three minute drink-and-
restroom break. As they finish, they group in two
lines near the drinking fountain. The teacher stands
at the head of the lines, making sure that the kids
are not goofing off. One of the fifth-grade boys in
line is gazing intently at a poster on a nearby wall
of different U.S. landmarks, and he turns to face his
teacher.

                    JOEY
          Mr. Z, where do geysers come from?

                    TEACHER
          Geysers?

The teacher's eyes flick to the poster where an image
of Old Faithful can clearly be seen near the bottom
right corner.

                    JOEY
          Yeah, how do they start?

                    TEACHER
          Well, geysers first start off
          as little boy-sers, and then
          they slowly develop to one day
          become fully-grown guy-sers...

The kids standing in line erupt into fits of
hysterical laughter. There is a short pause from the
boy before his face splits into a huge grin.

                    JOEY
          And when they get old they
          become 'geezers' and get stinky,
          like my grandpa, right?

The teacher smiles back.

                    TEACHER
          Yep. [Pause] And that's something
          for you to look forward to one day.

Fade to black.

"It's a little sad that today's youth don't get to experience a red rubber dodge ball to the face like we did back in the day."

— Abe

Belly Dancers and Roller Derbies

FADE IN:

EXT. EAST SIDE OF SCHOOL - MORNING

The teacher is standing outside near the parent drop off. Students walk by him on their way to various doors to await their teachers or play with friends. A few parents drop off their children and wave. The teacher waves back and smiles. After a few moments, a fifth-grade boy climbs out of his mom's car and approaches his teacher. He is smiling broadly.

>   JOEY
>   Good morning, Mr. Z.

>   TEACHER
>   Morning Joey, what's up?

The boy grins.

>   JOEY
>   Guess what *I* did this weekend.

>   TEACHER
>   No idea... maybe found a herd
>   of unicorns?

The boy chuckles.

>   JOEY
>   No, that was *last* week.

>   TEACHER
>   Well, I'm glad to see that
>   you lived to tell the tale.

>   JOEY
>   Me too. [Pause] I went to a...

The boy's voice drops deeply, and he throws his arms out dramatically.

>   ...roller derby!

>   TEACHER

                    A roller derby?
                              JOEY
                    Yeah, those things are *so*
                    educational.

                              TEACHER
                    And all this time I thought
                    it was just a bunch of women
                    skating in circles knocking
                    each other down... kind of like
                    fighting your way through a shoe
                    sale at Payless.

The boy adamantly shakes his head.

                              JOEY
                    There's SO much more to it,
                    Mr. Z.

                              TEACHER
                    Oh, really?

The boy nods enthusiastically.

                              JOEY
                    Yeah, it starts out with the
                    two guards skating into the crowd.

The teacher cuts the boy off.

                              TEACHER
                    Holy Hannah! Were you hurt?

There is a pause; the boy looks totally confused.

                              JOEY
                    Why would I have gotten hurt?

                              TEACHER
                    Well, you said the women skated
                    into the crowd.

                              JOEY
                    No, the group they skate into **that**
                    they're playing against... that's
                    the crowd.

                    TEACHER
          So you were playing in the
          game? Wow, that's so amazing,
          Joey!

                    JOEY
          No, I was in the crowd.

                    TEACHER
          Yeah, just like I said.

                    JOEY
          I wasn't in *that* crowd.

                    TEACHER
          So, just where were you?

                    JOEY
          I was in the crowd on the
          bleachers.

                    TEACHER
          They skated up into the
          bleachers? Man I had it all
          wrong... roller derbies are
          amazing!

                    JOEY
          No, they don't skate into
          the bleachers. None of the
          women were on the bleachers.
          [Pause] Well, a few of them
          were there, because they got
          hurt.

                    TEACHER
          I would only imagine that they
          would be hurt, you know, skating
          up into the stands like that.
          You are so lucky because
          you. should. be. dead.

The boy takes a breath to explain and then shakes his
head with an exasperated look on his face. The
teacher looks expectantly at the boy, trying hard not

to laugh.

                    JOEY
          Okay.
[breath]
          This is the ring.

The boy moves his hand over the flat top of one of
the three-foot rounded metal posts near them to try
to get the teacher to visualize what he's talking
about.

                    TEACHER
          Man, but those women must have
          been small to skate in a place
          that size.

                    JOEY
          No, we're just pretending that
          this is the ring they skated on.

The teacher says nothing and the boy continues.

                    JOEY
          So they skate this way -

[motions with his hand one direction]

          where the crowd is — not the
          crowd on the bleachers — the
          crowd playing the game.

The teacher still says nothing, and the boy goes on.

          So, they try to get through
          the crowd to score. And if
          they do, they get a point.

Pause.

                    TEACHER
          So, it's kind of like Quidditch?

                    JOEY
          Yeah.

                    TEACHER

Wow, they're flying on brooms?

                    JOEY
[Exasperated]
          NO, Mr. Z!

The teacher is fighting against the urge to break out
laughing.

                    TEACHER
          Joey, what I'm wondering is
          what in the world were you
          doing at a roller derby in
          the first place?

                    JOEY
          Oh, my mom and I got free
          tickets because my grandma
          is a belly dancer in the
          halftime show. We went to
          watch her perform.

There is a stunned silent beat.

                    TEACHER
          You're kidding.

                    JOEY
[Shaking his head]
          Nope.

                    TEACHER
          So let me get this straight;
          you and your mom go to roller
          derbies because your grandma
          is a belly dancer?

                    JOEY
          Yep.

                    TEACHER
          You have no idea how weird
          that sounds when you say it
          out loud...

                    JOEY
          It might be weird, but it
          sure was fun.

                    TEACHER
          You just might want to keep a
          lid on that little informational
          gem, Joey.

Fade to black.

"The worst part about coming to a new class is not knowing any of the other kids. The best part is making new friends."

— Jan

The New Student

FADE IN:

INT. CLASSROOM - MORNING

The teacher is getting the math lesson ready for the
day when a young boy enters the classroom. He pauses
at the door for a second and scans the room. Upon
noticing the teacher, the boy begins to walk towards
him.

                    JOEY
          Hi, you're Mr. Z, right?

                    TEACHER
          Joey, you know exactly who
          I am.

                    JOEY
          Oh, no I don't. You see, I'm
          a new student.

The teacher feigns surprise.

                    TEACHER
          Oh. Well in that case, what's
          your name?

                    JOEY
          Joey; it's spelled J-O-E-Y.

                    TEACHER
          Well, it's nice to meet you,
          Joey. So, is there anything
          I should know about you?

The boy looks thoughtful for a second, and then
cracks a whisper of a smile.

                    JOEY
          Yeah, I'm a slacker.

The teacher grins.

                    TEACHER

Well, now *that* is some important
information.

                    JOEY
I thought you would want to know.

                    TEACHER
Yeah, though I probably would
have eventually figured it out
on my own.

                    JOEY
Yeah, probably...

Fade to black.

"Literature responses would be a lot more fun if my teacher would let me do them on the Calvin and Hobbes books."

— Jesse

Literature Responses

FADE IN:

INT. CLASSROOM - MORNING

The students are in the classroom working on assignments. As the teacher works with three or four students at the back table, a boy at a nearby desk addresses him.

                    JOEY
          Mr. Z, literature responses
          are on Monday, right?

                    TEACHER
          Yep.

                    JOEY
          Good... I was thinking about
          doing mine on the math book.

Pause.

                    TEACHER
[Unbelievingly]
          The *math* book?

                    JOEY
          Yeah.

                    TEACHER
          Now, you do realize that you'd
          have to read the *entire* book
          to do a response on it, right?

                    JOEY
          The *whole* thing?

                    TEACHER
          Yep, words, numbers and all.

Pause.

                    JOEY
          Maybe I'll pick another book.

                    TEACHER
          Good idea. [Pause] By the way,
          what were you planning to do
          for a project?

                    JOEY
          I was thinking of drawing pictures
          of the different math symbols and
          showing them to everybody.

                    TEACHER
          Because that would be so much
          fun for everyone else?

                    JOEY
          Yeah, I thought they'd like it.

                    TEACHER
          Probably as much as getting
          their gums scraped.

The boy laughs.

Fade to black.

"I'm so glad that I'm in the fifth grade. This is the first time I've ever been this old before."

— Stephanie

Unspoken Thoughts

FADE IN:

INT. CLASSROOM - LUNCHTIME

The teacher **is** seated at the back table working on
grades and eating his lunch at the same time; a
fifth-grade boy slips into the room. The teacher
looks up in surprise because it's only been two
minutes since he'd dropped his class off at the
lunchroom.

                    TEACHER
          Did you even *chew* the food?

                    JOEY
          Yep.

                    TEACHER
          Well, you're back so quickly,
          I wondered if you just sucked
          it down.

The boy grins and heads back to the table. He flops
into a chair and then leans on his arms on the
tabletop.

                    JOEY
          Mr. Z, I'm tired.

                    TEACHER
          Nice to meet you, Tired, I'm
          Mr. Z.

Speaking in a swanky, deep voice like Joe Cool and
flipping his head to the side with a 'gun' finger
point.

                    JOEY
          Ooooooh yes, *you* are...

The teacher sits for a silent beat.

                    TEACHER
          You know, that was just the
          tiniest bit creepy.

The boy now begins speaking in his normal voice.

                    JOEY
          Well, what can I say? I'm a
          weird kid.

                    TEACHER
          I didn't say that.

                    JOEY
          I know, I did.

Pause.

                    TEACHER
          However, I have *thought* it a
          lot of times...

The boy breaks into laughter.

Fade to black.

"Hot dogs are just bologna before someone ran them over."

— Trevor

Wasp Paste, Juice, and Hot Dogs

FADE IN:

INT. LUNCHROOM - NOON

The teacher is sitting with his class at one of the
tables eating lunch. He takes a container of milk
from his Superman lunchbox along with the rest of his
lunch items. One of his fifth-grade students sitting
across from him is eyeing the semitransparent
container suspiciously.

                JOEY
     Mr. Z, what's in that container?

                TEACHER
     This? Oh, it's awesome juice.

                JOEY
     Really? It looks like milk
     to me.

                TEACHER
     Okay, you caught me; it's really
     liquid mayonnaise.

The boy grimaces.

                JOEY
     Eeewwwww.

                TEACHER
     Don't you like mayonnaise?

                JOEY
     I love mustard... mustard
     sandwiches.

The boy licks his lip. After a moment he looks
thoughtful.

                JOEY
     Hey, what's mustard made from,
     Mr. Z?

                TEACHER

                    Wasp paste.
The boy grimaces again.

                         JOEY
               But it tastes so good.

                         TEACHER
               Don't even think to ask me
               what hot dogs are made out of.

Pause.

                         JOEY
               Why, is it gross?

                         TEACHER
               You could say that.

                         JOEY
               I'll stick to the wasp paste.

                         TEACHER
               Well, it beats barfing up a
               lung.

                         JOEY
               Is that what hot dogs are made
               of?

                         TEACHER
               Trust me, you don't want to
               know.

Fade to black.

"I hate to compete against people who are better than I am, I want them to have a challenge."

— Samantha

Competitions

FADE IN:

INT. CLASSROOM - MORNING

The teacher has just finished meeting with his second
reading group during centers time. As the kids move
back to their desks, he readies to call the next
group up as a fifth-grade boy approaches. The boy
sits down at the table and speaks with a low, demonic
voice.

                    JOEY
          Meeestor Zeee.

The teacher looks up in surprise.

                    TEACHER
          Holy cow, what in the world
          was *that*?

The boy begins speaking in his normal voice.

                    JOEY
          That was my devious voice.

                    TEACHER
          Your devious voice?

                    JOEY
[Voice a bit higher than usual].
          Yep.

                    TEACHER
          Wow, and you have a wussy voice,
          too.

Pause.

                    JOEY
          Hey!

The teacher chuckles.

                    JOEY
          Mr. Z, do you know who's more

awesome than you?

                    TEACHER
          I'm sure there are lots of peop—

The boy cuts him off.

                    JOEY
          Two of you!

                    TEACHER
          Two of me?

                    JOEY
          Yep.

                    TEACHER
          Well, I'm glad that there's only
          one of me... I don't want to have
          to compete against myself.

Pause.

                    JOEY
          Yeah, because you'd *always* win.

Fade to black.

"If I was an animal I'd want to be a tiger, but right now I'm seven."

— Rob

Defense Mechanisms

FADE IN:

INT. CLASSROOM - MORNING

The teacher has just called up his second reading
group. Five kids get up from their desks and move
over to sit at the kidney-shaped table as the teacher
passes out their books on reptile defenses. As the
kids open their books, the teacher begins a
discussion on some of the defenses they read about
the day before.

>   TEACHER
>   So what defense have you guys
>   been the most impressed with
>   so far?

>   GIRL 1
>   I think that having poisoned
>   fangs is a great way to protect
>   yourself.

>   GIRL 2
>   Yeah, that's probably the best
>   protection.

>   BOY 1
>   The camouflage of some lizards
>   and snakes is pretty cool.

>   BOY 2
>   It's weird that some lizards'
>   tails come off so they can get
>   away.

>   JOEY
>   I love the lizard that shoots
>   blood out of its eyes; it's
>   *awesome*!

There is a pause for about two seconds before the boy
starts to make squirting noises and pantomimes liquid
shooting out of both of his eyes. The entire table is
silent for a beat; the other students and the teacher

all look wordlessly at the boy.

                    TEACHER
          Joey, that is *so* creepy.

                    JOEY
          You know what, Mr. Z? It sure
          would be cool if you could do
          that, too.

                    TEACHER
          What, shoot blood out of my eyes?

                    JOEY
          Yeah, but pepper spray!

                    TEACHER
          Now why in the world would I
          want to do something like that?

                    JOEY
          Well, you know... to spray the bad
          kids in class.

Pause.

                    TEACHER
          I think I'd prefer anti-kid juice.

                    JOEY
[Nodding]
          And then you'd spray the whole
          class with it, right?

Pause.

                    TEACHER
          Nope. I think I'd need it for only one
          student, Joey.

Fade to black.

"When somebody locks a door, it's time to start looking for a window."

— Amanda

Locked Rooms

FADE IN:

INT. CLASSROOM - AFTERNOON

The teacher has released his students for the day. As
he walks to the front of the room and starts to get
ready for the next week, he **notices a fifth**-grade boy
lingering behind in the classroom.

> JOEY
> Mr. Z, I'm sorry about talking
> so much in class today. I know
> that's why you sent me to the
> time out desk.

> TEACHER
> Well, you do know that I still
> like you, right?

> JOEY
> Yeah.

Pause.

> TEACHER
> You know, deep in my heart I
> have a little room that has the
> name 'Joey' engraved on the door.

> JOEY
> Really?

> TEACHER
> Yep, I keep it locked.

Pause.

> JOEY
> Yeah, you have to contain that
> ferocious and dangerous monster
> that's living in there, right?

> TEACHER
> Well, I have to keep myself safe
> Somehow...

Pause.

                    JOEY
          You better add some extra locks.

Fade to black.

"The best thing about Christmas is when there's a new layer of white frosting covering everything outside."

— Michael

The Greatest Gift

FADE IN:

EXT. FIFTH GRADE DOOR - MORNING

The teacher is picking up his class from outside. As
the students file past him and walk down the hallway,
one fifth-grade boy pauses for a minute.

                    JOEY
          Mr. Z, I was just wondering;
          what do you want for Christmas?

                    TEACHER
          I don't need anything, Joey,
          but thank you.

                    JOEY
          No, I mean it; what do you
          really want?

                    TEACHER
          I just want you to be the best
          you that you can be, Joey. That
          would be the greatest gift you
          could ever give me.

Pause.

                    JOEY
          But I want to buy you something,
          Mr. Z.

                    TEACHER
          Joey, really, I don't need you to
          buy me anything.

The boy gives a sly look and gives a knowing look.

                    JOEY
          What if I told you I have *eight*
          dollars?

                    TEACHER
          Then I'd tell you to save it.

Pause.

                    JOEY
          But what could I give you
          for Christmas then?

                    TEACHER
          Like I already said... just do
          your best. That's the best
          present you could ever give me.

The boy pauses and thinks for a second. A moment
later his face bursts into a smile.

                    JOEY
          I think I'll wear a bow on my
          head when I come to school
          tomorrow. I'm going to be the
          best present you've ever gotten!

Fade to black.

"The worst Christmas is when I woke up and realized that I was no longer a child. The best Christmas was the same one... it was watching the children open their presents."

— Josh

The Gift

FADE IN:

INT. CLASSROOM - MORNING

The students are just starting their classroom
Christmas party and are excitedly playing the games
planned by several of the mothers. As the kids rush
about the classroom with their oranges on white
plastic spoons, Joey's mom approaches the teacher.

                    JOEY'S MOM
          I just needed to tell you
          that I took Joey to the
          dollar store the other day
          to do his Christmas shopping.

                    TEACHER
          Oh, that can be a lot of
          fun. How'd it go?

Joey's mom drops her voice so she cannot be overhead.

                    JOEY'S MOM
          It went really well; he brought
          his own money and I just let
          him go around the store, getting
          gifts for all of his siblings—
          and for you.

The teacher glances at the package of peanut brittle
on his desk with Christmas well-wishing from Joey
written on a tag of demented-looking elves. He turns
back to Joey's mom as she continues.

                    JOEY'S MOM
          Well, we got out to the car
          and he started to pull things
          out of the plastic bags –
          he wanted to show me everything
          he'd bought for everyone...

Joey's mom stops and a smile creases her face as she
glances at her son, who is now devouring a plate of
nachos at his desk.

                    JOEY'S MOM
          He pulled out his sister's present;
          guess what it was?

The teacher, knowing this boy all too well realizes
that he has absolutely no idea. Joey's mom continues.

                    JOEY'S MOM
          He bought her a toilet plunger!

                    TEACHER
[Somewhat speechless]
          A what?

                    JOEY'S MOM
          A toilet plunger! I turned to
          him and said, "Joey, why on
          earth did you buy that for
          your sister?!" Do you know
          what he said?

The teacher shrugs.

                    JOEY'S MOM
          "It's for her potty mouth."

The teacher breaks out laughing as Joey's mom
continues.

                    JOEY'S MOM
          She doesn't really swear, but
          she says a lot of words to
          make her feelings clear. Joey
          decided that a plunger is
          exactly what she needed to
          take care of it. And to think,
          he thought up her gift all by
          himself!

                    TEACHER
          I'm not surprised. How do you
          think she's going to react on
          Christmas morning when she
          opens it?

                    JOEY'S MOM

                        137

[With a chuckle]
>   Well, I don't know about her,
>   but the rest of us will sure
>   get a good laugh.

CUT TO:

INT. CLASSROOM - AFTERNOON SAME DAY

The students getting ready to leave for their
Christmas break. The bell sounds and the teacher
dismisses them. Joey lingers for a moment at his
desk. His teacher approaches him.

>   TEACHER
>   So, a plunger?

>   JOEY
[Grinning]
>   It's what she needs, so I
>   thought I'd get it for her.
>   After all, she could really
>   use it.

The boy shoulders his backpack, gathers up his candy
from the party, and heads out the door offering a
"Merry Christmas!" as he departs. The teacher stands
for a moment or two more before shaking his head and
laughing.

Fade to black.

"I remember when I was a child, watching the snowflakes drift from the sky on cold, wintery days—each a perfect little crystalline creation. Then I'd go out to shovel the driveway and dump them all in a great, big pile."

— Jason

The Tongue Dilemma

FADE IN:

EXT. PLAYGROUND - MORNING

A few slivers of snow fall from the grey morning
skies as a fifth-grade teacher makes his way outside
for before-school duty. The online thermometer he'd
read earlier that morning had a reading of fourteen
degrees Fahrenheit. A few of the teacher's students
wander over from time to time to talk. One of the
girls, Becky, excitedly approaches.

                    BECKY
          Mr. Z, I just stuck my finger
          on the pole over there and a
          bit of the skin came off!

The teacher glances over to the four, four-foot poles
around the fire hydrant where a young boy is milling
about.

                    TEACHER
          Now that was pretty smart
          wasn't it?

                    BECKY
[Giggling].
          Probably not.

                    TEACHER
          You know what, Becky? You should
          have stuck your tongue to the
          pole... now THAT would have been
          REALLY smart.

Becky laughs and walks back toward the poles as the
teacher is asked a question by another student. A few
moments later, Becky comes running back to the
teacher, her voice full of frantic concern.

                    BECKY
          Mr. Z! Mr. Z! Joey's stuck to
          the pole!

The teacher, thinking that a joke is being played on

140

him, turns slowly with a doubtful expression.

> TEACHER
> Oh, really? Is he now?

> BECKY
> No, seriously... look!

The teacher gazes in the direction the girl is pointing and sees Joey with his tongue attached to the blue pole. The teacher bolts over to where the boy is flailing his arms and trying to communicate.

> TEACHER
> [Directed to the closest kid].
> Ryan, get to the nearest teacher's classroom and get a glass of the hottest water you can! GO! NOW!

The boy breaks into a run towards the school, along with two or three other students following along in his wake. The teacher turns his attention back to the boy who is trying to talk. A shudder passes though the teacher's spine as visions of A Christmas Story and The Watsons go to Birmingham 1963 fly through his head. It's just all so surreal; even watching the movie cannot have prepared him for this particular moment.

> RANDOM STUDENT
> [Approaching with a group]
> Hey, Mr. Z, what's going on?

> TEACHER
> Nothing! Get over there, now!

The teacher points to the other end of the playground. The student and the four or five members of his entourage slowly move away, still trying to catch a glimpse of the tongue-tied boy.

> TEACHER
> Joey, just why in the world would you stick your tongue on the pole?

> JOEY
> Youh thold meh tooh, Misthur Zeh.

141

                    TEACHER
          What do you mean, I told you
          to?

                    JOEY
          I huhrd youh thell Bekhee
          thut iht's thmart thoo puth
          yoh thung onth thuh phool.

                    TEACHER
          Joey, I was joking. Doing
          something like this doesn't
          make you cool.

The boy now has a long sliver of drool hanging down
from his bottom lip. His tongue is sticking out a bit
farther as he continues trying to communicate with
the teacher.

                    JOEY
          Ayh haff thoo goh thoo thuh
          bahthroon.

                    TEACHER
          You've *got* to be kidding me.

Several more students who approach are instantly sent
away by the teacher, who realizes that the last thing
the boy needs is a crowd watching him in this
particular dilemma. Instead though, a crowd is
forming about thirty feet away carrying on with
whispered conversations and pointings, like a herd of
gazelles stopping to watch as one of their members is
ripped apart by a lion in the Serengeti.

The teacher holds the boy's face firmly in one
position so that the end of his tongue doesn't rip
off. The drool trail is nearing ground level at this
point and is starting to freeze in midair. A lower
section of it catches on the pole and becomes
instantly frozen into place. The teacher wipes the
dribble from the boy's lip and starts to talk to him
so that he doesn't freak out.

                    TEACHER
        Don't worry, Joey. Everything's
        going to be all right. Just
        keep your head close to the pole
        and we'll get you out of this, okay?

                    JOEY
        I'hm thuck.

                    TEACHER
        Yeah, you can say that again.

After another minute or two, the boy finally realizes
the full extent of the predicament he's in and starts
to cry a little; the teacher keeps trying to console
him. *Lucky Lookies on the distant sidelines keep
trying to catch a glimpse of the dilemma taking
place. The teacher wonders if he should leave the boy
and go for the water himself. He changes his mind
several times.

A few moments later, Ryan comes hurrying out of the
school with a large cup of steaming water. The boy
gives it to the teacher who pours it over the pole.
Joey pulls at his tongue, stretching it out and
snapping it free of the pole's icy grip. The teacher
shudders again as he imagines a ripping sound as the
boy's tongue whips back into his mouth. The teacher
puts his arm around the boy's shoulder and leads him
into the school past troves of onlookers. The boy is
told to head for the office and the bathroom.

CUT TO: EXTERIOR. AFTERNOON. PLAYGROUND.

The teacher heads out for after-school duty in the
same spot. As he arrives, he notices the Joey looking
around the pole he was attached to earlier that
morning.

                    TEACHER
        Joey, what in the world are
        you doing?

                    JOEY
        I was just seeing if I could
        find the piece of my tongue that
        came off this morning.

                        143

                    TEACHER
          A piece of your tongue?

                    JOEY
          Yeah, the end of my tongue
          came off and I was just seeing
          if it was still attached to
          pole.[Pause]. I wanted to keep
          it.

                    TEACHER
          Okay, now that's just gross.

                    JOEY
          And cool, too...

                    TEACHER
          Well, I'm glad to know that no
          brain cells were lost.

                    JOEY
          Nope, just my tongue.

The teacher shakes his head and walks away.

Fade to black.

*Lucky Lookies: Those people who, at the scene of an
accident, stop and stare hoping to catch a glimpse of
something terrible.*

"My job as a first-grade teacher would be so much easier if seven year-olds would just act like mature, rational adults."

— Abe

Just Checking

FADE IN:

INT. CLASSROOM - LATE MORNING

The class is returning from the Science rotations at
the other fifth-grade teachers' classrooms. As the
kids file back to their desks, the teacher is
approached by one of his students.

>   JOEY
>   Mr. Z, do my eyes match
>   my shoes?

>   TEACHER
>   What?

>   JOEY
>   My eyes. I was wondering
>   if they matched my shoes.

The teacher looks down at the boy's shoes - black
with green stripes - and then back up at his brown
eyes. As he opens his mouth to answer to the boy's
question, the boy feigns a look of shock and his
voice takes on a tone of disbelief.

>   JOEY
>   Mr. Z... were you just
>   checking me out?

The teacher stands for a silent beat as the boy
breaks into laughter.

>   TEACHER
>   Nope, I was just trying to
>   decide which orphanage to
>   send you to.

Fade to black.

"For the first six or seven years I was a teacher, I pretended to have an identical twin brother. Sometimes, I'd take a 'sick day' and he'd come in to substitute. The kids could never figure out how he already knew so many of their names."

— Jason

Mistaken Identities

FADE IN:

INT. CLASSROOM - AFTERNOON

The teacher is having a few students call home before
heading off to remedial classes if their math
assignment was not completed. Three students are
waiting to use the phone. One boy, waiting at the
back of the line, waits his turn. After a few
minutes, he picks up the receiver and dials a number.
The teacher is getting a few items ready as the rest
of the class is transitioning to their other groups
and overhears the boy's side of the conversation.

                         JOEY
[Spoken into phone]
                    Hi, Mom, it's me. *[Pause]* I
                    didn't finish my math assignment
                    today when we corrected it,
                    and I was told that I had to
                    call home to let you know.
                    [Pause]. I didn't have time to
                    finish it all last night.
                    [Pause]. I wanted to, but I
                    got busy. [Pause]. Okay. [Pause].
                    Okay. *[Pause]*. Yeah, I love you,
                    too.

The boy hangs up the phone and then stands for a
moment, staring at the receiver. He looks somewhat
bemused. By this time, the most of the class has
filed out and the remedial group has started to enter
the classroom.

                         TEACHER
                    Joey, is something wrong?

                         JOEY
                    My mom said I should have
                    gotten my homework done.
                    [Pause]. She also said that
                    I'm grounded for two weeks.

                         TEACHER
                    Oh, I'm sorry to hear that,

148

but you know you really should
have gotten it done.

Pause.

                    JOEY
     Mr. Z?

                    TEACHER
     Yeah?

                    JOEY
     I think I dialed the wrong
     number... I don't think that
     was my mom.

                    TEACHER
     What was that?

                    JOEY
     I said, I think I called the
     wrong number. When I was talking
     to that lady I was thinking she
     was my mom, but then I think that
     maybe she wasn't. I think I mixed
     up two of the numbers and dialed
     the wrong house.

The teacher is trying hard not to start laughing, and
also not to also show a look of complete shock at the
same time. Somewhere, there is a boy who has just
been grounded for two weeks and who will arrive home
from school for the surprise of his life.

                    JOEY
     Do you think I should try to
     call her again?

                    TEACHER
     No, I think you've done enough
     damage for one day, you'd better
     get to class.

The boy hurries off after his classmates as the other
students take their seats and the teacher begins the
lesson.

CUT TO:

EXT. FIFTH GRADE DOOR - MORNING - NEXT DAY

The bell has rung. The teacher walks to where his
class is lined up to bring them inside to begin the
school day. Upon seeing Joey, the teacher remembers
the phone call from the day before. As the students
begin to file into the school, the teacher pulls the
boy aside.

                    TEACHER
          Joey, did you call the right
          number after all?

                    JOEY
          No, Mr. Z, when I got home,
          I asked my mom and she said
          I didn't call her. I guess
          I talked to somebody else's
          mom yesterday.

A few classmates that heard him making the call the
day before start whispered gasps of horror amidst
comments of, 'He called the wrong mom!' and 'Another
kid got into trouble!' The teacher sends these
students into the school building.

                    TEACHER
          So, I guess another kid got
          into trouble instead of you
          then, eh?

                    JOEY
          Yeah.

                    TEACHER
          Bummer for him.

                    JOEY
          Yeah, but I guess it could
          have been worse.

                    TEACHER
          Really? How's that?

                    JOEY

My mom could've grounded me,
too.

Fade to black.

"My Favorite things? Well, I could start off with 'raindrops on roses' and all the rest, but let's be honest here. My favorite things cost just a little bit more than any of those."

— Mandy

Favorites

FADE IN:

INT. CLASSROOM - MORNING

The teacher is walking back into the classroom from
making copies before school starts. A lone boy is
sitting at the back table with his Math book cracked
open. He is working on an assignment as the teacher
moves to the table.

                    TEACHER
          Hey, how's my favorite Joey
          in the whole, wide classroom?

The boy looks around the room, noticing that he is
the only kid currently present.

                    JOEY
          Mr. Z, I'm the only Joey in
          the room... in fact, I'm the
          only kid here.

The teacher puts on a knowing look.

                    TEACHER
          Ah, but that does not negate
          the fact that you're my
          favorite Joey!

The boy lets this sink in for a moment; after a few
seconds he looks up at the teacher.

                    JOEY
          Mr. Z, what if I were the
          only kid to show up for the
          day? Wouldn't that be cool?

                    TEACHER
          Yeah, it would. We'd have
          to go on a field trip, maybe
          go see a movie or something.

                    JOEY
          There's nothing I want to
          see right now.

                    TEACHER
          Then maybe we'd just have to
          stay in the classroom and do
          homework all day.

                    JOEY
          With you? Just you and me?
          THAT would be so awesome…

There is a pause as the teacher and boy both continue
to work on their individual projects.

                    JOEY
          Mr. Z?

                    TEACHER
          What?

                    JOEY
          Thanks for letting me be
          your favorite Joey in the
          whole, wide classroom.

                    TEACHER
          You betcha... after all –
          you could have been my
          second favorite Joey.

Pause.

                    JOEY
          Yeah, and you're pretty
          nice like that.

                    TEACHER
          Somebody's gotta do it...
          it might as well be me.

Fade to black.

"School's out! Let the brain shriveling games begin!"

— Matthew

<u>Brains</u>

FADE IN:

INT. CLASSROOM - AFTERNOON

The students are heading out to recess as the teacher
gathers up a few papers to take to the workroom to
make copies of; as he walks out the door, he notices
he's being followed by a fifth-grade boy.

                    TEACHER
          Did you need something, Joey?

The boy shakes his head.

                    TEACHER
          Then why don't you go out for
          recess? You only have fifteen
          minutes, you know.

The boy keeps in stride with the teacher as they move
down the hallway.

                    JOEY
          I was wondering something,
          Mr. Z.

                    TEACHER
          Sure, what is it?

There is a longish pause as the boy considers his
question. The teacher stops and looks intently at the
boy.

                    TEACHER
          Is everything okay, Joey?

The boy nods his head.

                    JOEY
          Yeah, I was just wondering...

The boy's voice trails off to silence and there is a
longish pause.

                    TEACHER
          About?

The boy casually leans in a bit and speaks quietly.

                    JOEY
          If you rolled your eyes
          back far enough, would you
          be able to see your own
          brain?

The teacher pauses to see if the boy is serious or is
pulling his leg; after a second he sees the hint of a
smile pulling at the corners of the boy's mouth.

                    TEACHER
          Wouldn't you have to have
          your brain with you before
          you start worrying about
          that?

The boy slaps a relieved hand to his chest and blows
out a relieved sigh.

                    JOEY
          That's a good point, Mr. Z.
          Thanks.

The boy grins and heads out the doors to the
playground.

Fade to black.

"We could all use more kissy-kissy scenes in our lives."

— George

The Assignment

FADE IN:

INT. CLASSROOM - LUNCH RECESS

Several students remain in the classroom, trying to get caught up on back work. The teacher is correcting and entering grades as he is approached by a student.

                    MARK
        Mr. Z?

                    TEACHER
        What did you need, Mark?

                    MARK
        I need math page P-6-14. The
        computer says I didn't do it.

                    TEACHER
        Did you check the extra
        assignment bin? I know that
        there were some there the
        other day...

The boy shakes his head.

                    MARK
        I already looked; there
        aren't any in there, Mr. Z.

                    TEACHER
        Well, I could print you a
        new sheet, but if I do, it'll
        cost you some class money.
        You remember that, right?

Mark nods as another boy stops working at his desk and turns his head.

                    JOEY
        You already did that
        assignment, Mark.

                    MARK
        I did?

JOEY
Yeah, I recognized your
handwriting on it, it's
in the 'nameless and orphans'
bin.

Joey springs from his seat and bounds across the
classroom to the blue, plastic tote clearly marked,
"Nameless and Orphans." He digs down under a few
sheets of paper and whips out the assignment.

MARK
Hey, that's my paper! I
just forgot to put my name
on it!

Joey grins, walks back to his seat, and begins
working again.

TEACHER
Hey, Mark... Joey just found
your assignment for you. You
didn't even tell him thanks.
You should be over there kissing
his feet right now.

At this statement Joey kicks off both of his shoes,
exposing exceptionally dirty socks. He spins around
in his chair, and holds his feet up for Mark to start
smooching them. Mark pauses and looks from Joey's
socks to the teacher, and then back at the feet
again.

MARK
Uh...

The teacher stifles his laughter and manages to
maintain a serious expression with quite a bit of
effort on his part.

TEACHER
On second thought, just go ahead
and take the paper. Maybe thanks
aren't really necessary after all...

JOEY

                    Curses.

Fade to black.

"I was horribly disappointed once when I discovered that the tooth fairy hadn't come by and paid me for my tooth. I went to my mother in great despair asking her why the tooth fairy hadn't come. She told me that my nasty breath had killed the tooth fairy and I would need to wait for the replacement fairy to come.'

—Jamie

The Tooth

FADE IN:

INT. CLASSROOM - AFTERNOON

The students are completing a team persuasive writing
assignment. The finished groups are instructed to
practice reading their picture books aloud with
voices and expression. The teacher begins to set up a
computer review on magnetism; a boy approaches the
teacher with his jaw shifted sideways and his head
tilted slightly to one side.

                    JOEY
          Mr. Z?

                    TEACHER
          What's up, Joey?

                    JOEY
          Would you pull my tooth out?

                    TEACHER
[Surprised]
          Excuse me? Did you just ask
          me to pull out one of your
          teeth?

The boy nods his head; he stares at the teacher with
a serious expression.

                    JOEY
          It's all wiggly and it bothers
          me; it hurts. This one here.

The boy opens his mouth and points to the lower right
lateral that he starts to move with his finger.

                    TEACHER
          And you want me to pull it out?

The boy nods his head jerkily.

                    JOEY
          Yeah. You could use those pliers
          in the supply closet if you wanted

163

to...

                    TEACHER
          I don't know…I'd really have
          to have your parent's permission
          before I started yanking all
          your teeth out.

                    JOEY
          Could you give me the pliers
          and I could do it myself?

                    TEACHER
          Joey, those aren't pliers,
          they're wire cutters.

                    JOEY
          Would they still work?

                    TEACHER
          Probably not, that is unless
          your teeth were made of wire.

                    JOEY
          So you won't do it?

                    TEACHER
          Sorry, I just can't start
          pulling our your teeth without
          a note from your parents saying
          that I'm allowed to do it...after
          all, what if I yanked the tooth
          and your brains came spilling
          out or something?

                    JOEY
          That wouldn't happen. I haven't
          had brains for a long time...

                    TEACHER
          Even so, I still need permission.
          Sorry.

CUT TO:

INT. CLASSROOM - NEXT MORNING

The students are working on the morning self-starter via the Promethean board. As the bell rings, Joey walks in. He sees the teacher at the back of the classroom and hurries up to him, grinning.

                    TEACHER
          So, did you bring the note?

                    JOEY
          Nope, I don't need to because
          my tooth is out now!

The boy points to the vacant place in his mouth where the loose tooth used to be.

                    TEACHER
          What happened?

                    JOEY
          Well, I decided to pull it
          out myself last night.

                    TEACHER
          Wow, so how'd you do it?

                    JOEY
          I decided to use the toaster.

                    TEACHER
          A toaster?

Joey begins to talk animatedly as he reenacts the entire episode from the night before.

                    JOEY
          I tied a loop on a piece of
          string and THEN hooked it
          around my tooth; THEN I tied
          the other end of the string
          to our old toaster…the one
          that doesn't work anymore.
          THEN I stood at the top of
          the stairs and threw the
          toaster down them!

The teachers instinctively puts his hand to his mouth, horror-struck.

                              TEACHER
                    So your tooth came out I
                    imagine?

                              JOEY
[Grinning]
                    Yeah, it flew right out, and
                    it jerked me forward a bit...
                    but I didn't fall down the
                    stairs though.

                              TEACHER
                    Well, thank goodness for that.

                              JOEY
                    Yeah, but now my tooth is out,
                    and it feels a lot better.

                              TEACHER
                    So now your tooth is 'toast'?

The boy starts laughing hysterically—after a moment
he becomes somber yet again.

                              JOEY
                    Yep, toast...with jam.

The teacher sighs, trying to seem disappointed.

                              TEACHER
                    Well, still I wish you'd have
                    brought that note.

                              JOEY
                    Tell you what, Mr. Z, you can
                    pull out the next one.

                              TEACHER
                    If only I could be so lucky.

Fade to black.

"I remember going to a friend's house when I was a kid. We were out in the pasture when he decided it would be funny to pee on the electric fence...

He never did that again."

— Jason

PEA SHOOTERS

FADE IN:

INT. CLASSROOM - AFTERNOON

The students are lining up to leave for P.E. As they
move to the appropriate lines, the teacher reminds
them that they are always to listen to other teachers
even more than they do to him. He then tells them
that they are all number one in his book and to make
him proud. Several students nod as they file out the
door; one of the boys lingers behind. As the last of
the kids leave the room, the boy turns to his
teacher.

                    JOEY
          Mr. Z, I have a pea shooter.

                    TEACHER
          Ewww, Joey, if you need to
          use the bathroom then just
          go. It's down the hallway
          and to the right.

The teacher points down hallway.

          Use the one that says little
          boys because if you walked
          into the girls' it would be
          embarrassing.

The boy stands, confused for a second before breaking
into fits of laughter.

                    JOEY
          Oh, I get it!

The laughter continues for several more moments.

                    TEACHER
          So, are you ready to head
          to P.E. now then, Muffin?

The boy nods his head with another giggle.

                    JOEY

Yeah.

Pause.

                    JOEY
        Mr. Z?

                    TEACHER
        What?

                    JOEY
        I feel glad that I'm number
        one in your book and
        not number two.

Fade to Black.

"Whenever I feel like I have far too many problems and that my life is hard, I find someone who has a far worse lot than I do. After watching them for a few moments I think to myself, 'Wow, I'm sure glad I'm not them'."

— Shawn

Problems

FADE IN:

INT. CLASSROOM - MORNING

The teacher is working with a ten year-old boy before
school. The boy has been having difficulty with
triple digit multiplication. While going over the
steps of multiplying, the teacher keeps calling the
boy back to attention when his mind starts to wander
or he starts talking about things off topic. After
nearly 30 minutes, the boy is only halfway done with
the assignment. The teacher stops and looks the boy
squarely in the eye.

                    TEACHER
          Have you noticed that I seem
          to want to get your homework
          done even more than you do?

                    JOEY
          Um... yeah.

                    TEACHER
          Now just why would that be?

The boy thinks for a second.

                    JOEY
          Because you're cooler than
          I am?

                    TEACHER
          Now what in the world would
          that have to do with homework?

                    JOEY
          I don't know...

                    TEACHER
          The truth is, Joey, I want
          you to be successful. Also,
          don't you feel better about
          yourself when your homework
          is finished?

                    JOEY
          Yeah, I do...

                    TEACHER
          Well, that's it. Plus, I care
          about you, too. [Pause]. Now
          look, you've got 22 minutes
          to finish your work before school
          starts... that's a lot of time.

                    JOEY
          Well, Mr. Z, I've got lots of
          problems.

                    TEACHER
          Yeah, you can say that again...

The boy giggles and then returns to work.

Fade to black.

"Some days I wish I didn't have to go to school. But some days I wish I was a tow truck."

— Herbie

The Confession

FADE IN:

INT. CLASSROOM - AFTERNOON

The school day is over. The clock above the dry-erase board reads 4:15. An 11 year-old boy and his teacher sit in a classroom. The boy has just finished his writing and is now starting on his Math homework. He pauses after a few minutes of working on his area and perimeter assignment. He then starts to work again. After a minute he stops. This goes on for a few minutes. Finally, the boy speaks.

                    JOEY
          Mr. Z?

                    TEACHER
          Yes?

The boy looks at his paper for a moment and then back at his teacher.

                    JOEY
          Did you know that there's only
          about five weeks left of school?

                    TEACHER

          That's what the office staff
          keeps telling me.

                    JOEY

          Well, I was thinking about that
          last night; I couldn't sleep.

                    TEACHER
          So, is this a good thing or a
          bad thing?

                    JOEY
          Well...

The teacher pauses in grading and looks at the boy
who is gazing intently back at him.

                    JOEY
          I'm gonna say something; I
          can't believe I'm going to
          say it either.

                    TEACHER
          Well, maybe you'd better
          not tell me then, some things
          are better left unsaid.

                    JOEY
          Yeah. [Pause]. Well, I'm
          going to say it anyway. You
          know, this is the first year
          I've ever had a teacher like you.

                    TEACHER
          Well, I certainly hope so.
          I'd hate to think that there
          were two teachers as good-looking
          as me running around.

The boy laughs for a moment and then becomes sober
again.

                    JOEY
          No, seriously. You're the first
          teacher I've ever had that I've
          ever been able to... connect with?
          Other teachers just didn't... well,
          they didn't understand me.

The boy stops and remains silent. A beat or two
passes. His teacher stops his correcting and looks at
the boy who is still staring back intently at him.

                    JOEY
          You're more than a teacher to me,
          Mr. Z. You're almost like a
          friend, too... a really good friend.
          I'm glad that you'll still be here
          next year so that I can still come
          and visit you when I'm in the sixth-
          grade.

The teacher sits speechless for a moment, and then speaks to the boy.

> TEACHER
> Thanks, Joey. Just remember though, I'm your teacher first, and *then* your friend. You still have to do your homework, too.

> JOEY
> That's okay, Mr. Z. I just wanted you to know.

Fade to black.

"You can pick your friends, and you can pick your wedgies. But if you pick your wedgies in front of your friends, you can bet you'll be hearing about it later."

— Melissa

Punishments

FADE IN:

INT. CLASSROOM – NOON RECESS

Only a few students remain in the classroom,
finishing up assignments. One boy approaches the
teacher, who is working on the day's Social Studies
assignment.

                    JOEY
          Mr. Z, do you know who's
          going to be in your class
          next year?

                    TEACHER
          Now, just why in the world
          would that matter to you?

Pause.

                    JOEY
          It just does. [Pause]. So,
          do you know who's going to
          be in your class?

                    TEACHER
          Yep, and I'm really excited
          to have you again.

The boy's eyes grow wide for a second.

                    OTHER STUDENTS
          Moted! Oooooh. You got that,
          Joey!

                    JOEY
          I get to be in your class
          again? That would be fun!

The teacher is a bit surprised.

                    TEACHER
          Really?

                         JOEY
              Yeah, I like to be punished.

Fade to black.

"How do they know if I called the wrong number?"

— Tanner

The Cellphone

FADE IN:

INT. CLASSROOM – MORNING

The class is working on their literacy tests. The
room is completely silent as the students answer
questions via laptops. Suddenly, there is a loud
outburst of noise from the area of the students'
backpacks.

                    BACKPACK
          ♫♪ What you gon' do with all
          that junk? All that junk
          inside your trunk? ♫♪

The class' attention is immediately snapped as one to
the rows of backpacks lining the south wall of the
room. The teacher stops helping a student with a
question and stands.

                    TEACHER
          All right, whose backpack
          is serenading us?

The class is completely silent.

                    BACKPACK
          ♫♪ I'm a get, get, get, get,
          you drunk; get you love
          drunk off my hump— ♫♪

                    TEACHER
          Anyone?

The teacher walks to the coat rack and removes the
cell phone that is singing even louder now that its
been removed from the shadowy confines of the
JanSport.

                    CELL PHONE
          ♫♪ My Humps, my humps, my lovely
          lady lumps; check it out! ♫♪

The class is trying very hard not to laugh, but

several giggles erupt from the corners of the room
anyhow. The teacher switches the ringer off and
glances at the phone display that reads, "mom.".

                    JOHN
          Hey, that's Joey's backpack!

                    BRENNA
          Yeah, then that must be Joey's
          phone, Mr. Z.

                    TEACHER
          Okay then class, get back to
          your tests. Joey, would you
          please come here for a minute?

The class still utters a few giggles as they return
to their laptops. Joey's face is burning red with
embarrassment as he approaches the teacher.

                    JOEY
[Whispered]
          Mr. Z, it's my mom's cell phone...

                    TEACHER
[Whispered back]
          Your mom has herself listed
          as 'MOM' in her own phone?

                    JOEY
          Uh...

The boy looks at the floor and whispers.

                    JOEY
          No, because it's not really
          her phone...

The teacher ponders this statement for a silent
moment, then raises his voice just loud enough for
the entire class to hear.

                    TEACHER
          Joey, the next time your mom
          lends you her phone, will you
          please make sure you turn the
          ringer off before you put it

                    in your backpack?

The boy grins and nods his head.

                         TEACHER
                    You can pick her phone up
                    after school.

                         JOEY
[Whispered]
                    Thanks Mr. Z.

The teacher gives a subtle wink as Joey returns to
his desk and recommences work on his test.

Fade to black.

"The funniest thing that happened today was when a boy in my class bit his tongue and asked for a Band-Aid. I laughed for 20 minutes while I watched him try and get it to stick."

— Abe

Real Men

FADE IN:

INT. CLASSROOM - MORNING

Most of the class is out of the classroom at PE. Only
four or five students remain working on incomplete
assignments. One boy, Joey, is staring at another boy
wearing a pink shirt, sitting a few seats away from
him.

                    JOEY
          Alex, did you realize that
          you're wearing pink?

Alex shrugs and glances down at his shirt.

                    ALEX
          Oh, yeah, I guess so... it's
          the only clean shirt I had
          left.

Pause.

                    JOEY
          Well, it takes a *real* man
          to wear pink!

                    ALEX
          Why aren't you wearing pink
          then?

Pause.

                    JOEY
          I don't *have* a pink shirt.
          My mom wouldn't buy me one.

Alex stares back at Joey for a second longer before
returning back to his work.

                    JOEY
          Hey, Alex, can I have your
          shirt?

Alex doesn't look up but instead continues to work.

                    ALEX
        Real men don't wear shirts...

Joey sits for second longer and then starts to
pretend to pull off his shirt.

                    TEACHER
[Warningly]
        Joey, keep your clothes on.

                    JOEY
        Sorry, Mr. Z, just trying to
        keep it real.

                    TEACHER
        Yeah, and so am I. Besides,
        real men do their homework.

Pause.

                    JOEY
        Well, it's a good thing I'm
        a kid then, isn't it?

Fade to black.

"We should always enjoy the moment in which we are currently living; there will always be time to look back and remember it with fondness."

—Jason

Diminishing Return

FADE IN:

INT. CLASSROOM - NOON

The class has gone to lunch and the teacher is
sitting alone in the classroom eating from a box of
Sundried Tomato and Basil Wheat Thins. After a few
minutes, the door opens and one of his students walks
in. The boy pauses by the door and then moves over to
the table where the teacher is sitting; he doesn't
say anything for a few seconds.

                    JOEY
          Hey, Mr. Z.

                    TEACHER
          Hi, Joey. What brings you
          back to my world?

                    JOEY
          It's cold outside so I thought
          I'd come back in and visit you.

Pause.

                    TEACHER
          You know, a better answer
          would have been, 'I just missed
          you, Mr. Z and I wanted to see
          you again. Also, it's cold outside.'

The boy looks thoughtful for a second.

                    JOEY
          Mr. Z, I just missed you and
          wanted to see you again.
          Also, it's cold outside.

                    TEACHER
          Oh, that's nice.

The boy is silent for a few seconds.

                    JOEY
          I'm gonna miss you, Mr. Z.

                    TEACHER
          Miss me?

                    JOEY
          Yeah, I just want to stay
          in your class. [Pause]. Hey,
          maybe you could follow me
          to sixth grade, then seventh,
          then eighth, and then on to
          high school and college. You
          could be my teacher every
          single year.

                    TEACHER
          I'm pretty sure you'd get
          sick of me, Joey. You'd also
          get tired of the way I teach
          after a while.

The boy adamantly shakes his head.

                    JOEY
          I'd never get sick of you,
          Mr. Z.

                    TEACHER
          Sure you would, Joey, it's
          all about diminishing return.
          Remember when we learned
          about that during our Market
          Day presentation?

                    JOEY
          You mean when John kept eating
          all those pretzels and then
          wanted water instead of more
          of them?

                    TEACHER
          Yep.

                    JOEY
          Not me, I'd just keep wanting
          more.

Silence.

                    TEACHER
          Well, then you'll need to keep
          visiting me here at school then,
          because I can't be visiting you...
          that would just be creepy.

Pause.

                    JOEY
          Mr. Z?

                    TEACHER
          Yeah?

                    JOEY
          Could I have a few of your
          Wheat Thins?

The teacher offers up the box and the boy takes a few
of them; he silently munches in the ensuing silence.

                    JOEY
          Do you think that I could
          just hang out with you again
          sometime?

                    TEACHER
          As many times as you want to,
          Joey, and for as many years...

Fade to black.

ADDITIONAL QUOTES

While I couldn't use all of the quotes I was supplied with for this little project, here are some that I felt well worth mentioning:

"Spare the dog. Kick the cat."

— Brent

"I don't understand cat lovers. I could personally never own a pet that sees me as its inferior."

— Gerberta

"Trying to hold a cat while drying your hair with an electric hairdryer is like running naked through neck-high patch of stinging nettles—it's just something you shouldn't do."

— George

"I have a theory about cats…
But, if I shared it, I'd have to kill you…
Before they do…"

— Melinda

"Why aren't my silver teeth worth more than my white teeth?"

— Brent

"Mom, the tooth fairy is lame. She's always at least a day late."

— Henry

"Teeth are one of the worst investments a person can make. You will never receive more quarters than you spend on paste, brushes, floss, rinse and dentists. It's a scam."

— Marc

"As I child I would lose a tooth, put it under my pillow and find a quarter waiting for me in the morning...now, as an adult I can't help but wonder just what does she do with them once they are hers?"

— Shawna

"Will the tooth fairy return my tooth if the other one doesn't grow back?"

— Brent

"You mean I'm supposed to tell my kids that there's a strange, magic woman who sneaks into their rooms at night while they're asleep every time they loose a tooth? Sounds kinda creepy..."

— George

"What happens when the tooth fairy loses a tooth?"

— Jamie

"Hilarity - that moment when you open your mouth to make a witty jest and find yourself shoving your foot in instead."

— Shawna

"Living the dream...maybe a nightmare, but a dream nonetheless."

— Bill

"I'm so tired of a life of danger."

— Owen

"Mom! Stop acting crazy like that. I only like it when you're really, super freaky. It's weird when you're just a little crazy."

— Herbie

"Can I be a robber for Halloween if I promise not to be one when I grow up?"

— Herbie

"What exactly does the tooth fairy do with all of those teeth? And why in the wide world does she give money for them? She must be crazy. And rich."

— Neve

"Hey sharks, you may have your own week on television, but cats have their own eternity on the Internet."

— Abe

"LISTEN TO WHAT I MEANT, not to what I said."

— Wendy

"Eli had a stick and it was wet and he got the wet on my shirt."

— Micah

"My six-year-old always makes a very compelling argument with, 'Nuh-uh dad'."

— Abe

"Mom and Dad won't miss me, they've got pictures."

— Zander

"Diminishing return is like the school year. The longer it goes, the less interest you have."

— Austin

"Did you know chickens poop?"

— Micah

"Whatever the prize is in a box of cereal, you can bet that it will be at the bottom. Turn the box upside down and open that side because nobody wants to have to eat all that cereal to get to it."

— Jean

"Never hold an umbrella and leap off of a roof. It doesn't work."

— John

AFTERWARD

Isn't this over yet? you ask. Nope, sorry. Fear not though Dear Reader, for this part promises to be quick and painless.

They say it takes an entire village to raise a child, and it takes a slew of people to pull off a book. It would be remiss of me to not include them in some way for all of the help they have been.

Firstly, to Miya Edwards, thank you for your work with format and editing the manuscript, as well as creating the wickedly entertaining Joey Dosen't Lyke Kittys logo. For those who have somehow failed to see this, I include it here for your enjoyment:

Joey Dosen't Lyke Kittys

Many thanks also go to Gerberta Black, for being a best friend to Jason, as well as ready with the red pen for manuscript edits. You and your family are absolutely amazing.

A heartfelt thank you to Melinda "Mindy" Durrant, who was always ready to edit, suggest, support, cheer on and be an all-around great friend to an author and his sister. I am so happy he brought us together.

To Kristen Randle, for her help with screenplay formatting help.

To Rachel Rubow, for her help with cover edits and helping to pick out just the right "Joey".

And finally, a big thank you to Britton Rees and the Rees family, for allowing Britton to be the face of "Joey".

ABOUT THE AUTHOR

September 9, 1970 – August 11, 2012

Jason Zimmerman was born in San Francisco, California, but spent the majority of his childhood in Summit Valley, Washington, which is where he began writing stories in his head. Later he would begin to jot these stories down on paper, and he wrote his first full-length story in the seventh grade. He had several manuscripts and spoke often of publishing children's books. *Moments with Joey* is the first of these books.

Jason was a third, fourth, fifth, and sixth-grade teacher in Provo, Utah where he won numerous awards for teaching excellence. He was a recipient of The Golden Apple, The Crystal Apple, was named the Provo School District Teacher of the Year, and was The Milken Teacher of the Year for the state of Utah. Jason loved teaching, and worked to create a safe, nurturing learning environment where he could help motivate kids to see the value of knowledge and hard work.

When Jason wasn't in the classroom, playing his guitar, hiking the lonely vast deserts of southern Utah, or running his photography business, he was usually writing at his blog, Adventures & Misadventures of Daily Living. It is here that he archived various moments with Joey, photographs he'd taken, and posted personal insights to life and the everyday moments thereof. You can find these posts at: http://teachinfourth.blogspot.com.